# Clash of East and West

The Persians

Imperial Greece

# The Rise and Fall of Empires

# Clash of East and West

### The Persians

### Imperial Greece

**Daisy More**
*The Persians*

**John Bowman**
*Imperial Greece*

CASSELL
LONDON

Authors: Daisy More, John Bowman
Picture Researcher, Janet Adams
Assistant Picture Researcher, Noreen O'Gara
Translator, Ilana D'Ancona

Consultants:
  Persia: Ali Banuazizi
  Greece: Judith Hanhisalo

Concept, Robert J. George
Design Implementation, Designworks


**Rizzoli Editore**
Authors of the Italian Edition:
  Introduction: Professor Ovidio Dallera
  Persia: Professor Anna Maria Guardasoni
  Greece: Dr. Flavio Conti
  Maps: Fernando Russo
Idea and Realization, Harry C. Lindinger
Graphic Design, Gerry Valsecchi
General Editorial Supervisor, Ovidio Dallera


CASSELL LTD.
35 Red Lion Square, London WC1R 4SG
and at Sydney, Auckland, Toronto, Johannesburg,
an affiliate of
Macmillan Publishing Co., Inc.,
New York.

© Rizzoli Editore 1980

First published in Great Britain 1980

ISBN 0 304 30573 1

Printed in Italy

# Contents

# Preface

Persia evokes images of a fairy-tale land. A sophisticated and slightly remote country, it has fascinated and contributed to other cultures for thousands of years. The distribution of Persia's gold mines, for example, influenced the route of Alexander's conquests, and the characteristic terrace structure of its buildings found expression in Greco-Roman architecture as well as in some roof-top gardens of today's skyscrapers. The bright colors and exotic customs of the Persian court also inspired the elaborate, incense-clouded ceremonies of the Byzantine court. Evidence of Persian etiquette can still be found in such time-honored rituals as the kissing of the shah's or the pope's feet. Even such domestic furnishings as portable couches and footstools are survivors of Persian nomadic customs.

Native talent and natural resources were seemingly inexhaustible in ancient Persia. Tendencies to stylization, meticulous craftsmanship, and an unbounded love of extravagence gave rise to superbly fashioned metal- and ivory-work, as well as delicately wrought jewelry and cylinder seals. Of course, the Persian legacy was far more than decorative. The ancient Persians showed a remarkable talent for organization and invention, and when they extended their reach to the Mediterranean and the borders of India, they transmitted their culture's achievements in agriculture, mathematics, and astronomy. In addition, Zoroastrianism—the exotic state religion of the Persians—set a precedent for the West, encompassing concepts of good and evil, salvation and perdition, and eternal reward and damnation. The prophet Zoroaster also advanced a belief in a savior and a final judgment—prefiguring, by hundreds of years, Christian doctrine.

But Persia is perhaps most often remembered as a culture that recognized the value of assimilation. The great Persian leaders, particularly the Achaemenid dynasts Cyrus and Darius, were adept at borrowing from and transforming the artistic achievements of other advanced cultures, not the least important of which was Greece—the nemesis of the Persian state. The cultural exchange between Persia and ancient Greece is all the more remarkable considering how different they were. The dissimilarities are no more clearly demonstrated than in the way each culture viewed its sovereign. In deference to his sovereignty, the Persian king of kings was deliberately isolated from his peoples by court ritual and pageantry. Yet the greatest of Greek leaders, Alexander the Great, mixed freely with his troops, showing compassion for their fears and pain. Even late in his career, when he proclaimed himself divine, Alexander could not disguise his humanity.

Unlike that of Persia, Greek culture always remained closely attached to the homeland, even when Greek had developed into an international language and when Greek dynasts ruled foreign kingdoms. Assimilation, in the case of Greeks, meant the adoption of the Greek way of thinking. The Homeric epics of the eighth century B.C. provide us with a detailed picture of early Greek life, in which individual achievement played as decisive a role as national pride. Indeed, the Greek experience was distinct in its struggle to explain the world in human terms. This revolution in attitude was already well developed by the fifth century B.C., when the philosopher Protogoras declared: "Man is the measure of all things."

Given the Greeks' passionate interest in all things human, it is no wonder that they created their gods in their own image. Unlike the remote and inaccessible gods of the ancient Egyptians or the Persians, the Olympians were close to the hearts and minds of the Greeks. However familiar and companionable, the Greek gods were set apart from man in one crucial respect—they were immortal. Nonetheless, the Greeks strove to bring man ever closer to divine favor, toward the immortalization of human achievement in art, drama, and poetry. The total man—his physical, intellectual, and spiritual being—was at once the inspiration and justification for Greek art and culture. Even the great stone temples, with their characteristic geometric purity, were derived from human proportions.

The tiny and nearly barren Greek islands gave rise to a miracle of human creativity, the effects of which are still very much felt. Art, drama, poetry, history, philosophy, mathematics, and, perhaps most important of all, a new vision of man, are our inheritance from classical Greece. For it was only once we had gained an understanding of and respect for man's innate capabilities that the concept of democracy as an inalienable right could be advanced.

# The Persians

This is the palace which I built at Susa. From afar its ornamentation was brought. . . . The gold was brought from Sardes and from Bactria . . . the precious lapis lazuli and carnelian was brought from Sogdiana . . . the ivory from Egypt and from Sind and from Arachosia. The stone cutters who wrought the stone, these were Ionians and Sardians. . . . The men who wrought the baked brick, those were Babylonians. The men who adorned the wall, those were Medes and Egyptians. Saith Darius the King: At Susa a very excellent [work] was ordered; a very excellent [work] was [brought to completion].

Thus did Darius, king of kings of the Persians, celebrate the creation of his magnificent palace at Susa

from the vast and varied resources of his realm. His pride was conspicuous but warranted. Darius the Great (558?–486 B.C.) was one of the most energetic and capable of the Persian kings who ruled the largest empire the world had ever seen, unsurpassed until Rome was at its peak. At its fullest extent, the empire encompassed three of the great gardens of mankind—the valley of the Indus in India, the Tigris and Euphrates in Mesopotamia, and the Nile in Egypt—as well as Asia Minor and the Greek cities.

Whenever possible, the Persians preferred to rule with a lenient hand, in part because they respected the cultural achievements of the people they conquered. Their subjects—numbering ten million or more—all paid taxes to the officials of the one king, used the king's coin, and housed the king's soldiers, but they were free to compile their own histories, speak their own languages, and worship their own gods. By granting considerable autonomy to their subject peoples, the Persian kings were able to forge an empire out of a confusion of variant customs and

*Preceding page, columns of the Hall of Audience of the royal palace at Persepolis, built in the sixth and fifth centuries B.C.*

*Hills rise (below) beside the upper reaches of the Tigris River at the northern end of the great Mesopotamian lowland plain, where intensive agriculture and urbanization began.*

*High above the Mesopotamian plain lies the upland Iranian plateau, ringed by mountains. On the northern perimeter, the loftiest peak of the Elburz chain is Mount Damavend (below left), which is visible from Tehran. Because the distant snow-covered peaks look blue, the ancients called the Elburz "the mountains of lapis lazuli." The peaks also block rain-bearing clouds from the Caspian, making the plateau exceedingly dry. Semi-desert (above) and desert lands (left) are widespread, in contrast to a subtropical strip north of the Elburz.*

cultures. The achievement was short-lived, lasting a mere two hundred years, but it survives as history's most creative experiment in rule by tolerance.

Of the empire's ten million people, only two million were Persians. The Persian homeland was in an obscure region called Persis, or Parsa (modern Fars), in the southwestern corner of the great Iranian plateau. This high plateau is ringed by the Elburz and Zagros mountains, and at its center are stretches of arid desert and of barren, brackish mud. The slopes of the mountains were more favorable to agriculture and, thus, to habitation. Indeed, long before the Persians came onto this plateau, it was the site of the earliest known husbandry. From about 7000 B.C. onward, the planting, sorting, and replanting of wild mountain grasses produced barley, wheat, and rye, while the selective breeding of wild animals created domesticated herds of goats, sheep, and cows. The early settlers on the mountain slopes dug tunnels and

pits underground to save snow in winter and floodwaters in spring. With this ingenious method of storing water, they were able to cultivate fruit-bearing trees. These early subsistence farmers eventually established a few towns that grew to considerable size, but the land was not sufficiently fertile to support a sizable agrarian population. It was west of the plateau, on the enormous flatland of Mesopotamia, where extensive husbandry and culture on a significant scale first developed.

Over thirty centuries before the rise of the Persian Empire, grains from the highlands were planted on the land between the Tigris and Euphrates rivers.

The inhabitants of this region—they called themselves the "black-headed people," and we call them the Sumerians—dug a network of water-storing canals to keep the dusty plains moist throughout the long, intemperate summer. They also built levees and wharves on the lower reaches of the rivers and large, walled cities of mud-brick.

The Sumerians chose kings for their cities whom they held to be the sons of gods, and they built towers, called ziggurats, to provide a place where the gods might descend and make contact with the people. One Sumerian city, called Uruk, was ruled by a king named Gilgamesh, who was to become the hero of the

*The streams that cut through the slopes of the thousand-mile-long chain of the Zagros Mountains to the west of the Iranian plateau provided water for man's earliest farming activity. A Zagros river turns to rapids (left) as it cuts through a valley whose hills were once forested. Steppe land on the inner Zagros slopes (below right) gave pasture where early inhabitants first domesticated animals. Camel caravans still follow old paths between steppe and desert. Right, the delta land along the Shatt-al-Arab—the channel formed by the confluence of the Tigris and Euphrates rivers that flows into the Persian Gulf.*

oldest written epic poem—the Sumerians were the first people to develop a written language.

In the third millennium, the cities of the Sumerians were united under one king. But this league fell in around 2370 B.C. to the Akkadians, Semitic migrants from the desert and the Mediterranean hill country in the west. The Akkadians settled farther upriver, in the region of the city of Babylon. Under them, control over the plain grew tighter.

By now, the great Mesopotamian plain to the west, called Edinnu (we know it as Eden), was a thriving and prosperous region. Here slaves labored with hoes, plows, and scythes. Doves and ducks, as well as sheep and cows, were raised for the table. Farmers grew dates and figs, and they fermented an intoxicating mead from honey. Grapes were pressed into wine, which was considered a choice gift of the gods. Dyers and weavers produced fabrics, and artisans worked with wood delivered on skin rafts from the upper reaches of the Euphrates. Metalworkers smelted and hammered goods later packed on boats or camels for trade. The indigenous people established schools, laws, and taxes, as well as kingships and organized armies. When the Persians settled in the mountains that rose at the edge of the Mesopotamian plain, they were in no position to overtake such powerful and civilized neighbors. It would take centuries for them to summon the strength.

The ancestors of the Persians were a group of people called the Aryans. The name "Aryan" means "lords," or "noblemen," and it is the Old Persian root of the word "Iran." Linguists have deduced the existence of an early common language they call Proto-Indo-European, basing their theory mainly on the existence of similar words in ancient Persian and Sanskrit (as well as others in Old English, Greek, German, Celtic, and Slavic). It is believed that Proto-Indo-European was spoken in the fifth millennium

B.C. or earlier, and that the Aryans, the last group thought to have spoken it, migrated to the area of modern Afghanistan sometime around the beginning of the second millennium B.C. This group of people eventually broke up, some going west to the Iranian plateau and the rest going east to the Indus valley. From the Indo-European vocabulary and from some of the songs recorded centuries later in Sanskrit, we can have a glimpse of the kind of life the Aryans lived in Afghanistan.

The Aryans themselves were probably descended from the people who first domesticated the horse on the grassy steppes of southern Russia. In perhaps the

# Mesopotamian peoples until 1600 B.C.

The Hittites came from the Hatti region (western Anatolia) in the second millennium B.C. and had their capital at Hattusa.

The Hurrians originated in eastern Mesopotamia in the third millennium B.C. In the sixteenth century B.C., they founded the kingdom of the Mitanni.

The Akkadians were a Semitic dynasty founded by Sargon in the second half of the third millennium B.C.

The Sumerians originally settled in southern Mesopotamia toward the middle of the fourth millennium B.C.

# Maximum Assyrian extension

The oldest known Assyrian capital was Ashur, founded ca. 2000 B.C. During the nineteenth century, the Assyrians were ruled by an Akkadian dynasty founded by Ilu-shuma and, during the following century, by an Amorite dynasty. After the Hittite invasion (1530 B.C.), the Assyrian civilization underwent a period of decline until the reign of Tiglath-Pileser I, who raised the empire to unprecedented heights. The new empire experienced further reorganization in the ninth century and reached its peak during the following two hundred years.

# Mesopotamia after the Assyrian decline

At the close of the seventh century, a new independent dynasty installed itself in Babylon and, in an alliance with the Medes, conquered Nineveh, thus bringing an end to the Assyrian Empire. This period, which continued up to the conquest of Babylon in 539 B.C. by Cyrus the Great, is called the Neo-Babylonian era.

The Median Empire, with its capital at Ecbatana, was founded by Deioces (728–675), whose son Phraortes (675–653) unified the divisive Median tribes. His successor Cyaxares (625–585), in an alliance with the Babylonians, contributed to the final defeat of the Assyrians in 612 B.C.

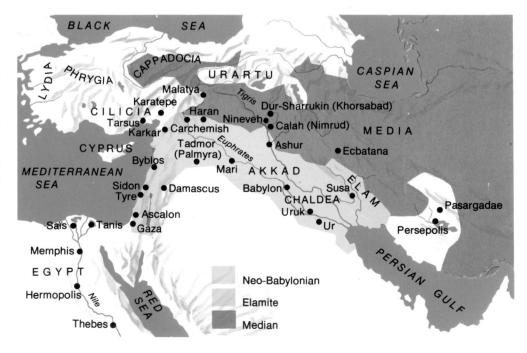

# The beginning of the Achaemenian Empire

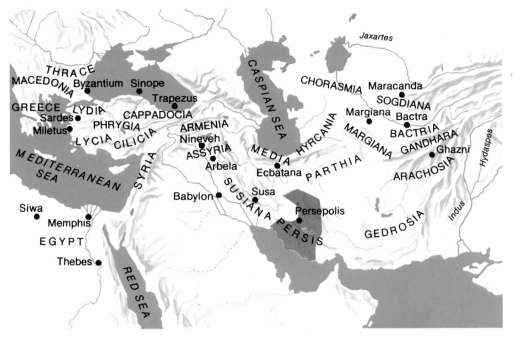

The Achaemenian dynasty, named after the ancestor of the dynasty, Achaemenes, had its origins in Parsumash, a southern region in Asia Minor on the Persian Gulf. Notable Achaemenians included Cyrus I, king of Anshan (ca. 640–600 B.C.), and Cyrus the Great, the true founder of the Achaemenian dynasty. Cyrus the Great was responsible for consolidating the Persian tribes that formed the original nucleus of one of the greatest empires of antiquity.

## The empire under Cyrus the Great

After declaring war on the Median king Astyages (his maternal grandfather), Cyrus conquered Ecbatana and, in 546 B.C., assumed the title of king of the Persians and Medes. The annexation of Lydia (546 B.C.) was the first in a series of conquests. Between 545 and 539, Cyrus subjugated several colonies in Asia Minor, then moved on to the Neo-Babylonian Empire. Because Babylon submitted peacefully, Cyrus allowed it cultural autonomy. Other conquests included Bactria, Sogdiana, and Margiana. According to Herodotus, Cyrus later invaded the region of the Massagetae, where he died in battle in 528 B.C.

## The empire under Darius

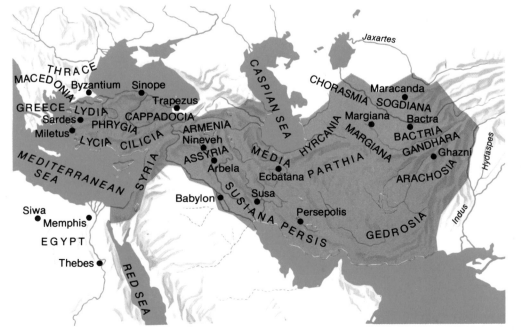

After assuming the throne in 521 B.C., Darius I had to subdue Babylonia, Susiana, and Media before he could organize his vast empire, which included Asia Minor and Egypt. The Persian Empire was divided into twenty satrapies connected by an efficient road system and a quick courier service. Darius was a brilliant leader, but failed in his ambitions to conquer the Athenians at Marathon (490 B.C.).

third millennium B.C., the Aryan lords rode their small fleet horses beside the Caspian and up the mountain passes onto the high plateau to the south. "Lead us to meadows rich in grass past all pursuers," they sang. These nomads had learned to herd cows, and they lived primarily on meat and dairy products. They did have, however, a rudimentary understanding of farming. The Aryans had also learned the uses of copper, and probably bronze, and they admired good metalwork.

One Aryan religious ritual was to slaughter a bull and cast its meat onto the fire, so its savory smell could rise to the gods—to the lord of the arching sky, to the heroic lord of thunder and rain, or to the lord of lightning and vital, sacred fire. The Aryans believed that the world was inhabited by both good and evil spirits. They also worshiped the lord of the moon, the lord of order, and the lord of truth—all three of whom kept a vigilant watch over all men to insure that they remained honest. Sometimes the Aryans sprinkled the beef with *soma*, a euphoria-producing juice pressed from the stalks of an unidentified plant

which grows in the mountains, but which is said to have originally been grown in heaven and brought to earth by an eagle. The soma that remained after each offering to the gods was consumed by the Aryans. It made them feel light and immortal, a prelude to the rewards worthy men could expect when they died and ascended to the house of song in the sky. There scarred warriors and wrinkled beauties would receive fresh bodies. The grim fate of the wicked was everlasting life in a dark, underground pit of hunger. But soma made all men feel brave, and moved them to courage in battle:

> With Bow let us win, with Bow, the battle.
> With Bow be victors in the sharp encounters.
> The Bow does to the foeman what he loves not.
> Bow-weaponed may we subjugate all quarters.

Eventually, Aryan warriors assembled horse-drawn war carts and chariots and plunged down the mountain passes of the Hindu Kush, driving out the local farmers and seizing their lands. These invaders became the people of India. After 1400 B.C., another wave of nomadic horse lords from beyond the Caspian began moving up onto the plateau. This time, they came armed with iron weapons. It took them generations to spread out and claim territories for themselves. One group of slim, olive-skinned Aryans, or Iranians, fought their way into a six-thousand-foot-high granite pass in the northwest part of the plateau near Ecbatana (modern Hamadan). They became known as the Medes. Another group took longer to settle, pushing farther and farther south, until they too came to rest on high ground. It was an inhospitable land, but they would say of it, "Soft lands breed soft men." They called it Persis, and they became the Persians.

The Medes and the Persians originally settled in

With an unusual location for its spout, this terra-cotta piece (far left) from Loristan in the Zagros Mountains shows the interest in animal forms common to pre-Persian and Persian craftsmen alike. Near left, a long-spouted tenth or ninth century B.C. terracotta pitcher from Tepe Siyalk, probably intended to resemble a bird, decorated with a male animal and geometric signs. With dark red ornamental motifs on a lighter background, this pitcher was too fragile for everyday purposes and may have been used to pour libations at prehistoric burial rites.

Above, a painted ceramic chalice from Susa, at the base of the Zagros Mountains, showing a wild goat or ibex whose curved horns enclose a geometric design. This work is typical of that done in the Zagros in the late fifth millennium B.C., several thousand years before the Iranians entered the area. Made of fine clay that was thrown on a slowly turned wheel, it is too porous to hold liquids. This proud stone statuette (right) comes from the region of Shiraz in southwestern Iran and dates from around 3000 B.C.

*The subtle differences between male and female were as intriguing to the ancients as they are today. In the terra cotta of a bull (above), the hump and horns are emphasized to demonstrate male power. Female power is asserted in the breasts and genitals of the terra-cotta figurine (below near right), perhaps put into an early tomb to aid the soul's birth. Both are from the ninth or eighth centuries B.C. and were found at Marlik, near the Caspian Sea.*

earth-walled camps near the indigenous people of the mountains and gradually adopted the habits of agricultural life. Cattlemen by tradition, they began to marry among the ancient farming stock of the Zagros Mountains. They too learned to raise sheep, goats, and pigs, and they found that, with care, they could save water for their grains and fruits in underground storage places. The mountain folk were of a variety of origins and had developed diverse customs. Some killed all individuals who lived past seventy, eating the men and burying the women. Some exposed the dead to the air or threw them to the vultures or the dogs, later collecting the cleaned bones in sanitary ossuaries. At Tepe Siyalk, the arrival of the Iranians is marked by a change from burial under the floors of

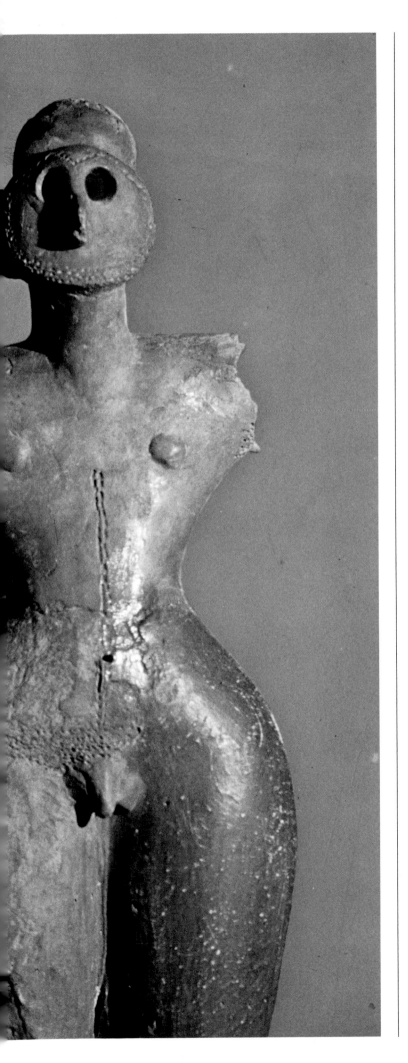

houses to interment in a necropolis, where the tombs were small wooden houses with double sloping roofs.

The merging of the farmers with the nomads did not always mean a triumph of nomadic customs. The bold, expressive Persians tried to copy the more sophisticated Elamites, who lived on the flat plains of Susiana at the base of the outer Zagros, where they had easy access to the Mesopotamian cities. In 1175 B.C., the king of Elam stormed the walls of Babylon and wrested the city from its overlords. He sent many trophies home to the Elamite city, Susa. Susa had always been a hub of roads and waterways, and it soon developed into a great city with a thousand men on the palace payroll.

Despite the refinements of Elamite influence, Persian life remained relatively rustic. The extended family provided structure, with the father ruling as an all-powerful patriarch. Family groups formed clans, and the head of a clan could ally his fighting men with those of other clans to form a tribe of roughly a thousand warriors. The Persian headmen began the practice of choosing one of their number as chief headman, or tribal king. These local kings built themselves mountain fortresses, and gradually, through custom, the kingships became more or less hereditary.

Of the several hundred tribes of Aryan and indigenous peoples scattered across the Iranian plateau, ten were the tribes of Persis itself. Four of these were composed of families who were still nomadic herders, three of farmers who had settled permanently, and three more of people who also worked the land and who were in the position to claim ownership. The Pasargadae (as the Greeks called them—"Parsagard" may have been the true name) were one of these three landholding tribes. Among them was a family—the Achaemenids—from whom it became customary to choose the tribal king. Like all Persian youths, the Pasargadae were taught from the age of five to shoot the short bow and wield a dagger. From age seven, they learned to break and ride a horse and to use

*This male terra-cotta figure (left) with pronounced genitals, beard, chest, and pubic hair comes from Tepe Tourang at the base of the Elburz Mountains, southeast of the Caspian. The masculine figure was of special importance to the herding Aryans, who came into this territory without a single goddess in their pantheon. On the following pages appear small, bronze figures of stags created in Loristan in the eighth and seventh centuries B.C.*

# Ancient Persian archaeology

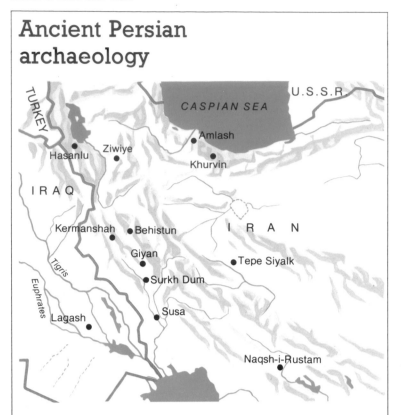

The map above locates various archaeological sites of the Persians and their predecessors. Hasanlu inhabitants made pottery in the second millennium B.C., and later, sheep- and cattle-raising Manneans worked metal. Amlash has produced remains from the ninth century B.C. which reveal an artistic individuality remarkably unaffected by Mesopotamian influences. Kermanshah, which has been recently excavated, is a cluster of Neolithic sites dating from 10,000 to 5000 B.C. Behistun is the site of the rock cliff on which Darius the Great had his history carved. Tepe Siyalk documents Iranian development from the second half of the fifth millennium B.C. through ceramics and other objects. Surkh Dum is where a number of Loristan bronzes have been found—most by local peasants—and is the only site where a scientific excavation of bronzes has been conducted. Susa produced painted pottery from the fifth millennium B.C. and was the capital of the Elamite culture. At Lagash, excavations have revealed the ruins of a palace, temples, and numerous inscribed tablets. Naqsh-i-Rustam, near Persepolis, is the site of the cliff tombs of the great Achaemenid kings.

*Below, two bronze bit ends for horses, from Loristan. Early herders rode their cows and great warriors rode bulls.*

weapons while on horseback. On prescribed days, they sat with the men to watch the sacrifice, drink what they now called *haoma,* and listen to songs of hard riding on otherwise forgotten steppes beyond the distant Caspian.

In the northern part of the plateau, in what is now the Hamadan-Tehran-Isfahan area, the Medes had formed half a dozen large tribes. In about 670 B.C., the six tribes pledged themselves to follow a single leader in hopes of protecting their land from the aggressive Assyrians, who had taken Mesopotamia from the Elamites and held it for almost five hundred years. Not content with occupying the plain alone, the Assyrians had hauled their battering rams to the Mediterranean and onto the Anatolian peninsula—present-day Turkey—and, closer to home, even up onto the Iranian plateau. They had stolen horses from the Medes, taken men as slaves, and put the Medes under their tribute system.

As the Persians had copied the Elamites, the Medes tended to copy the Assyrians, especially in the manner in which they treated their king. Like the Assyrian king, the Median king, or *khshayathiya* (from which the word "shah" comes), was no rude chieftain. The khshayathiya claimed to hear the voices of the gods. He showed his face only to a select few and expected other men to prostrate themselves before him when they were invited into his presence. His feet, from which a mighty power was believed to emanate, were not allowed to touch the ground but rested honorably on a special stool.

Shortly after the Medes chose their first king, the whole area of the Mesopotamian plain, the adjoining Anatolian peninsula, and the Iranian plateau were threatened by a new wave of savage Indo-European horsemen from the pasture lands between the Danube and the Volga. In the third quarter of the seventh century B.C., these Scythians and their relatives, the Cimmerians, depopulated many of Assyria's tribute-paying towns. The Median king, Cyaxares, was forced to pay tribute himself to some of these hordes. He finally managed to poison several of their leaders at a feast and then joined with many of the remaining Scythians to attack the already weakened Assyrians. Cyaxares and the Scythians also had an invitation to meet with a rebel governor in Babylon, a potential ally who wanted to free his province from the Assyrian oppression. The Median king and the Babylonian governor, Nabopolassar, met in 612 B.C. According to the official Babylonian chronicle, they then "marched upstream on the embankment of the Tigris and pitched camp against Nineveh. From the month Simanu till the month Abu, three battles were

The bronzes of Loristan are representative of nomadic art: everything had to be portable, and it is to such objects that the craftsman applied his skill. The ritual bronze ax (near right) has a hand grip and a blade on which can be seen the figure of a man clasping a fish. The ax was probably never used for battle but was designed for the grave as a symbolic weapon for a dead warrior. All the Loristan bronzes were found in a necropolis, and the axes in the trove were fanciful adaptations of more usable forms extending back as far as the third millennium. Two bronze daggers and a sword (far right) were each made from a single piece of metal and were probably used for more earthly battles. Loristan daggers were often enriched by silver and ivory inlays in the handles. Below, a boss from a bronze shield with a winged figure at its center. If the Loristan bronzes were made by Indo-European-speaking Cimmerians who settled in the Zagros early in the first millennium, as is thought, these pieces may be among the last creations of the Bronze Age. Iron came into common use in 1000 B.C., bringing an end to bronze work for all but ritual purposes.

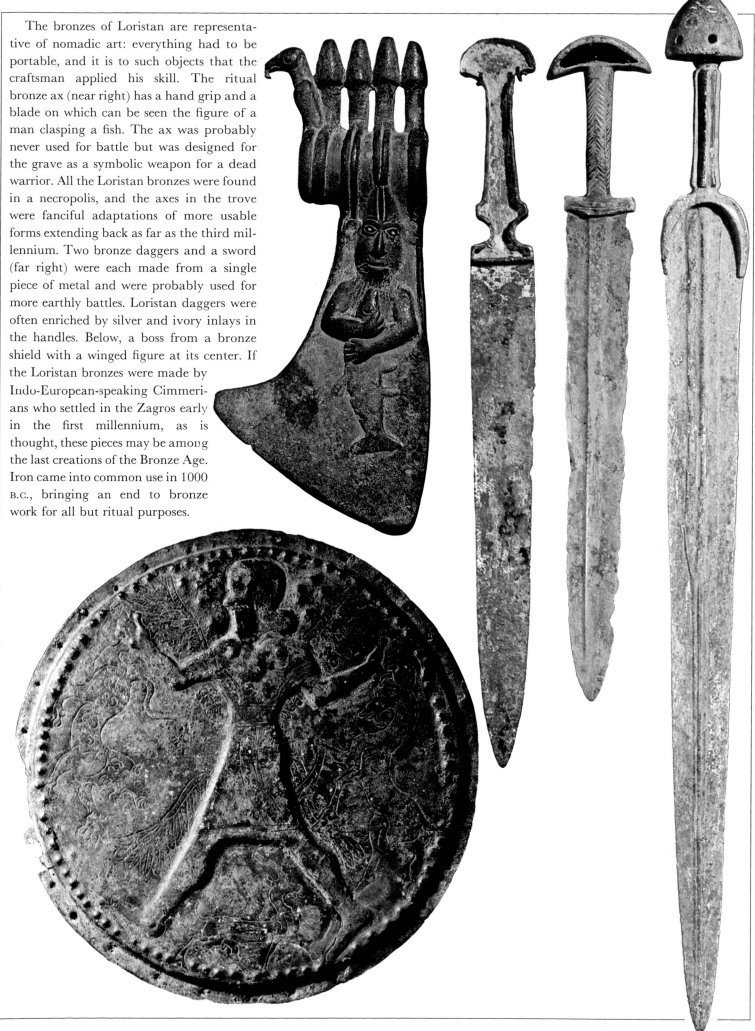

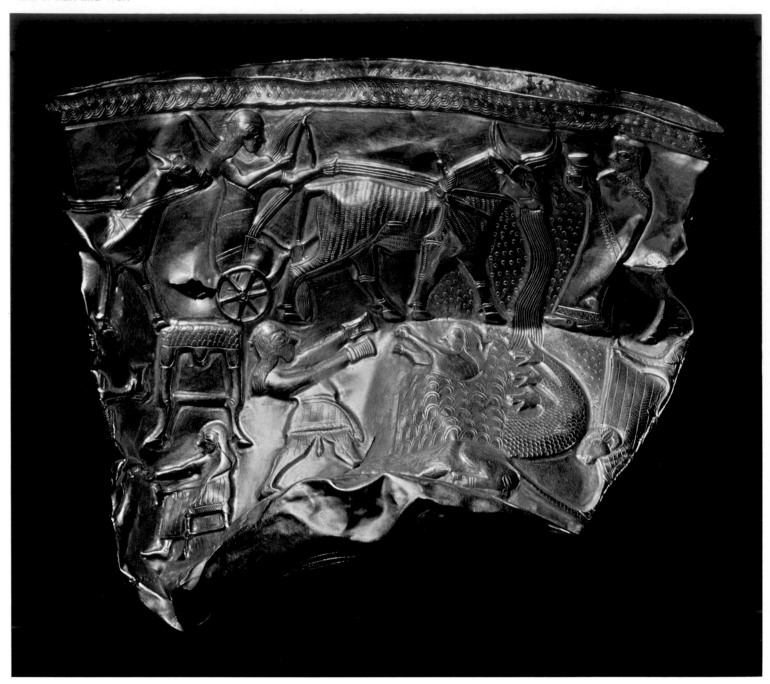

fought, then they made a great attack and . . . turned the city into ruin hills and heaps of debris."

King Cyaxares triumphantly ordered a great palace to be built atop a hill in Ecbatana. Seven concentric walls were constructed up the narrowing peak,

*Gods in their chariots ride across the top of this large golden bowl (above), while below them a hero fights a mountain god. The eleventh century bowl was discovered during excavations at the ancient fortress at Hasanlu next to the bodies of three warriors in Caucasian dress. We know that men from the Caucasus destroyed the fortress about 800 B.C. and can imagine that these three met their deaths trying to make off with the bowl. The ninth century golden cup (left) for Kalar Dasht shows lionesses both in profile and in the round.*

and the many-colored palace dominated the summit. Cyaxares demanded and received tribute from many of the Iranian tribes on the plateau, including the Persians. To make good his claim that he would control the northern half of the Assyrian domains while Nabopolassar secured the southern, he sent his soldiers through the mountains in a well-calculated show of strength.

The Urartu of Armenia promised tribute, as did the Cappadocians, who lived at the neck of the long peninsula of Anatolia that ran west toward Lydia. But wealthy Lydia put up a five-year fight until a solar eclipse in May of 585 B.C. frightened both sides into a premature truce. A Lydian princess married Cyaxares's son, bringing a short-lived peace to the Medes. Cyaxares organized his lands into a system of provinces, using local people as governors. Wherever he traveled, he built hunting gardens, called paradises, in which, like the Assyrian monarchs before him, he could shoot game flushed by attendants.

In 575 B.C., when Cyrus—or Kurush, as the Persians called the founder of their empire—was born, Persis was a lowly vassal to the Medes. Cyrus is believed to have been the son of Cambyses, a tribal king of Persis. Each year Cambyses sent a tribute to the king of the Medes. In 575 B.C., the king was Astyages, the prince who received a Lydian princess as wife to seal the Median-Lydian truce. By another marriage Astyages had a daughter who is believed to have become the wife of Cambyses—in another political alliance—and the mother of Kurush.

Cambyses was tribal king of only half the Persians, since his father, Cyrus I, had received but half a kingdom from *his* father, Teispes, who had given the other half to another son. The boy Kurush may have grown up with the idea of reuniting Persis. Most certainly he was taught to ride and shoot; when his father died, Kurush was appointed captain of a group of fifty or a hundred in the training army in which all Persian youths served. He became Cyrus II, and in about 559 B.C., by a precocious

*A female figure (right) on a silver cup from Hasanlu looks over her shoulder. Her dress is decorated with stylized flames, and beside her is the star sign that often identified a deity. Hasanlu was probably occupied by Manneans at the time this cup was made, who are thought to have descended in part from the Hurrians of the second millennium. The shape and type of decoration on the objects found at Hasanlu indicate affinities with the art of Loristan, but Assyrian stylistic influences are also in evidence.*

blend of charm and threat, the young chief appropriated his cousin's half of Persia. He was sixteen at the time.

Within ten years, Cyrus had Media too—long the strongest nation in Asia—in an equally bloodless coup. Such carefully arranged, diabolically quiet takeovers were the mark of this empire builder. It is not certain exactly how Cyrus managed it, but it is known that his grandfather, Astyages, sent a counselor named Harpagus and some soldiers to his ally Babylon to complain about some Babylonian excursions too close to Median territories. Harpagus never got to Babylon but instead took himself and his soldiers through the highlands to Cyrus. The aged grandfather then rode some four hundred miles over mountain roads to lead his soldiers against Persis. Cyrus waited with his men on the plain of Murghab for battle, but Astyages was quietly delivered in chains to his grandson, who treated the deposed king well. Cyrus is said to have founded his capital city Pasargadae on the field of this victory, some thirty miles northeast of the later site of Persepolis.

The year was 550 B.C. Cyrus climbed into his grandfather's royal chariot and traveled north to claim the royal treasury at Ecbatana. There, the Medes pledged their loyalty to Cyrus: the officials, whom he permitted to keep their jobs; the landlords, who sent him tribute (which amounted, under later kings, to 450 talents of silver, 100,000 sheep, 4,000 mules, and 30,000 horses annually); the Magi, a powerful tribe of priests; and the officers of the Median army. Governors of the far-flung Median provinces sent hasty messages of loyalty as well. Cyrus called himself "king of kings," adopting the Median title. He was twenty-five years old.

At the time, Babylon was the largest and greatest city in the world. "I have made the city of Babylon to [be] the foremost among all the countries and every human habitation," its best-known builder, Nebuchadnezzar, boasted. Thousands of slaves had built his palace, Babel, which soared above the other buildings of this city of a million people. Only the ziggurat of Esagila, the great temple of Babylon's chief god Bel-Marduk, surpassed the palace in height and splendor. Popularly known as the Tower of Babel, the ziggurat had a base one hundred yards on a side, its seven stages rising to a height of three hundred feet.

In the streets, the city's turbaned citizens walked, each wearing a seal around his wrist embossed with his name. There were rich landholders, commoners, merchants, and artisans, and thousands of slaves who, instead of wearing their names around their wrists,

*The gold figure (facing page) of a man holding a* barsom, *a sacred bundle of thornless branches, appears on a plaque from the Oxus treasure. This collection of objects, dating from the seventh to fourth centuries B.C., was found in 1877 among the remains of what may have been a temple on the Oxus River in Afghanistan. The gold armlet (top) was once inlaid with gems; it shows horned griffins, imaginary creatures with the heads and wings of eagles and the bodies of lions. The tiny four-inch, horse-drawn toy chariot (immediately above) may have been a gift from the Persian king Xerxes to his favorite son.*

# Let it be written on stone

Most of the inscriptions the Achaemenids ordered written upon stone or metal were rendered in the wedge- or nail-shaped cuneiform signs that had been developed far earlier for impressing words into clay. The Sumerians invented writing about 3000 B.C., and for over three thousand years, the cuneiform graphic system was used throughout the Middle East for writing languages that differed widely among themselves: Sumerian, Elamite, Akkadian, Babylonian, Assyrian, Urartian, Hittite, and later, Persian.

Sumerian was similar to Chinese in that it was composed of monosyllabic units grouped together: the word "to nurse," for instance, might be made of stringing together "grown-girl-give-milk." This kind of agglutinative language lent itself to having a single mark represent a single word-unit. Gradually, the pictures became stylized, wedge-shaped marks, whose size, angle, width, and combinations corresponded to specific meanings.

When the Semites of Akkad took over the Sumerian cities, they modified the old characters to express a quite different kind of inflected language. The Assyrians took over the Akkadian symbols but soon adopted the far simpler phonetic script of Syrian businessmen called Aramaic. This writing required learning fewer than thirty signs—in contrast to the thousands cuneiform demanded.

Cyrus spoke Persian, cut his inscriptions in Elamite and Babylonian, and had his dispatches put cursively into Aramaic on parchment. It was Darius who "dignified" Persian by having a cuneiform system of some 3,607 signs made for it. The script was dubbed Old Persian.

*The cylindrical seal of King Darius (above) shows his name vertically in cuneiform script in three languages: Persian, Elamite, and Babylonian. Like the rubber stamp signature of today, the king's seal could be used by underlings. When rolled over wet clay, the seal imprinted a scene of Darius in his chariot taking aim with bow and arrow. His arrows pierce one lion while another lies wounded. In both depictions above, the winged symbol of the Persian god Ahura Mazda hovers over the king, offering divine protection.*

*In a trilingual inscription of a gold plaque (left), found in the stone foundations of the Hall of Audience at Persepolis, Darius attributes the formation of the Persian Empire to the will of Ahura Mazda and invokes the god's blessing for eternity. In a detail from an Assyrian bas-relief showing the hand of a winged cupid holding a bucket (above), superscribed cuneiform letters represent the sounds of the Assyrian language. This relief was found at Nimrud and dates from the ninth century B.C. Cuneiform is, in general, made up of wedge- or nail-shaped marks, read from left to right, whose size, angle, width, and combinations correspond to specific meanings.*

Above, cuneiform characters scratched into the eastern stairway of the Hall of Audience at Persepolis. Shown about one third of its actual size is one of many prisms (right) on which the Assyrian kings inscribed their historical records. This eight-sided example relates the feats of Sargon II.

Left and in detail below, the seven-foot basalt stele of the Babylonian king Hammurabi inscribed with the famous code, ca. 1760 B.C. Hammurabi's 282 laws, written in Akkadian cuneiform on the stele, appear beneath a relief of the king and the sun god, Shamash. With flames at his shoulders, the god sits on his throne, holding the regalia of divine power—the baton and the ring—and dictates the laws to the earthly king.

# King of kings

Few speak kindly of the Assyrians. This Semitic-speaking people came into power on the upper Tigris in the twelfth century B.C. Their primary god was Ashur, the god of war. With their battering rams, their siege towers, and their new iron weapons, the men of Ashur took the cities of the plain, and their king adopted the Akkadian title "king of the four corners of the world." Then they rode their armored horses toward the Mediterranean.

Standing outside a city, the Assyrians would demand submission. If it wasn't forthcoming, a special contingent of soldiers would dig under the city's walls and set timber burning, while the "artillerymen" maneuvered the battering-rams. When the city had surrendered, the Assyrian monarch would take a seat on his portable throne inside the ruined walls and decide who should live and who should die. Enemy captains might be sacrificed to Ashur or impaled or flayed and their skins put up on the walls. Simple soldiers might be taken into the Assyrian army, while artisans could expect slavery and began to pack for travel. Then the images of the town's gods would be hoisted onto Assyrian shoulders, and the people would gather behind what carts were left for the trek into exile.

Tiglath-Pileser III (746–727 B.C.) raided Media on the Iranian plateau for horses and men, taking some 65,000 down to the plain as slaves, replacing them with some 15,000 Arameans whose cities he had bro-

The firm gaze of Ashurnasirpal II (883–859 B.C.) still commands awe (left). This head, from Nimrud, Ashurnasirpal's capital, is part of the sole perfect statue in the round that archaeologists have unearthed in Assyria. The titles of the king are inscribed around his chest. Sitting on his throne, Ashurnasirpal would have let his countenance be glimpsed only from a distance by subjects prepared to kiss the floor at his feet.

Below left, the walls of Nineveh. It was Sennacherib (705–681 B.C.) who boldly named his residence at Nineveh "the palace without rival." The walls of its more than seventy halls and rooms were sculpted with reliefs depicting his victories. Below, a detail from the Black Obelisk of Shalmaneser III (858–824 B.C.) showing Israel's king Jehu on hands and knees before the Assyrian king. Winged Ashur, the national god of Assyria, looks on.

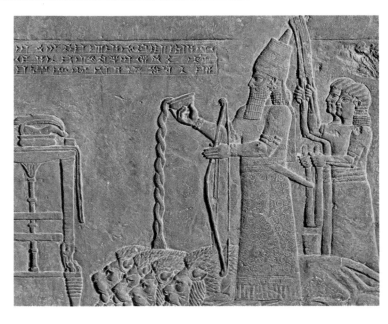

*Ashurbanipal (668–627 B.C.) astride a horse (top) calmly thrusts his lance into the mouth of a clawing lion. This bas-relief (ca. 650) was found at Nineveh. Immediately above, Ashurbanipal pouring a libation over four dead lions before an altar. The cuneiform reads in part: "I, Ashurbanipal, king of hosts, king of Assyria, whom Ashur and Belit have endowed with might, slew four lions."*

*Right, King Sargon II (722–705 B.C.). Sargon's slaves undertook construction of a capital in the vicinity of Nineveh, on the site of modern Khorsabad, where this alabaster bas-relief was found. He dictated his dispatches to the Syrians, Egyptians, Elamites, Urartians, and Babylonians in Assyrian, but his scribes translated them into the more simply written Aramaic script of Syria.*

ken, "making them look like hills of ruined cities over which the flood has swept."

Farther north were the sturdy Urartu of the Armenian mountains who raised cattle, sustained large irrigation works, and supported a "king of kings." Soon, the Assyrian monarch had this title, too. The Assyrians moved onto the Anatolian peninsula for more towns.

A thousand miles to the south lay the warm land of Egypt. When the Assyrians marched into the capital of Memphis, their king Esarhaddon (681–669 B.C.) said "I am gigantic, I am colossal. I am without equal among kings." Thebes was sacked and the Assyrians temporarily engulfed the Nile valley. The towns of Egypt were assigned tribute and told to make sacrifice to Ashur and the great gods. If the Assyrian monarch was becoming king of kings, the chariot-riding Ashur was as fast becoming god of gods.

When Ashurbanipal (669–629 B.C.) was building his library at Nineveh and drawing up his long list of vintage wines, raiding nomads were making trouble to the north and rebellion was threatening in Babylon. The king who loved books had to go to war. Ashurbanipal regrouped the army,

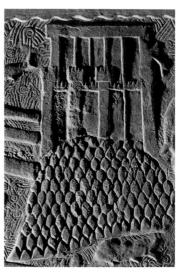

*A detail (left) of Sennacherib's siege of the city of Lachish in Judea in 701 B.C. The Assyrian king ordered the walls of his palace at Nineveh decorated with scenes from this, and other, victories. In the tower over the gateway stand four soldiers of the city with weapons, who hurl down stones and flaming torches. The Assyrians are moving a siege engine up, the ramming points of which can be seen to the left. Through the door in the tower men and women rush out— one of whom is visible here—carrying their possessions. Out of view to the right, three men are being impaled.*

*Above, Assyrians attacking an island fortress, possibly a Phoenician city. In this scene from the walls of Sennacherib's palace at Nineveh, the two-storied buildings typical of those in Phoenician cities can be seen. To reach an island, the Assyrians would load their chariots onto boats, make their horses swim, and then cross on inflated skins.*

*Left, the fortified city of Lachish. When the city had been captured, the Assyrians moved on to Jerusalem, of whose king Sennarcherib reported: "As to Hezekiah, the Jew, he did not submit to my yoke, I laid siege to forty-six of his strong cities, walled forts, and to countless small villages. . . . I drove out 200,150 people, young and old, male and female, horses, mules, donkeys, camels, big and small cattle beyond counting."*

An Assyrian horseman (right) as depicted in Ashurbanipal's palace rides past palm trees with his lance at the ready. Such details as the palm helped palace visitors envision the glories of the landscape over which the monarch reigned. The horseman wore a tunic, boots, mail armor, and a helmet pointed to repulse blows. For a saddle he employed a blanket or a piece of leather and he always rode without stirrups.

Two Assyrian archers (below) pull at bows of medium length and curvature. In the positioning of their arms can be seen the enormous strain involved in drawing the bow. Archers were paid in plunder from the abandoned stores and houses of the cities they helped break.

bringing together the lancers, the charioteers, and the cavalry and abandoning the old system of sending men into battle by village or blood bond. He marched southeast into Elam, where he razed the ziggurat at Susa and drove the Elamites, their cattle, and even the dug-up bones of their kings back to Assyria. He ignored the poor remote Persians over the Zagros, after they had sent him a hasty message of submission. When Ashurbanipal died, there was unrest throughout the empire. In a few years Babylon rose under its own rebel ruler, Nabopolassar, who brought together the Medes and the raiding Scythian nomads to the north. The three went against the Assyrian Empire, bringing down Nineveh in 612 B.C. By 605 B.C., Ashur no longer rode his chariot across the world.

The monumental art of the Assyrians was on the same scale as the military might of the empire and the grandiose pronouncements of the kings. Enormous palaces were flanked by huge temples and high ziggurats, and all was surrounded by powerful protecting walls. Assyrian artists excelled at sculptured relief, only rarely attempting sculpture in the round. Even the enormous winged monsters which stood guard at Assyrian palaces were actually done in high relief on stone slabs, giving the sculpture an architectural function and even greater weight and mass than it already possessed.

*In this ivory relief (left), a warrior from the palace of Shalmaneser III at Nimrud wears the chain armor that Shalmaneser introduced to his warriors. Above is the smiling female face that has been dubbed the "Mona Lisa of Nimrud." It was carved around 720 B.C. from an ivory tusk that must have been very large, as the head is almost six and a half inches across at the top. The piece is designed to be used as a mask, hollow in the back.*

*Below, a wounded lioness, in one of the most realistic hunting scenes from the lion-hunt bas-reliefs at the palace of Ashurbanipal. Blood streams from the wounds of the dying lioness who, though partially paralyzed, drags herself howling toward the hunters.*

*Made of limestone and almost fourteen feet high, this winged, human-headed bull (below) was one of a pair designed to keep enemies away from the eighth century B.C. palace at Khorsabad. The bull has a fifth leg which makes it appear to be standing still from the front, though in movement from the side.*

Taureau ailé à face humaine
(Gardant l'entrée d'une porte du palais de SARGON (VIII° siècle))

bore the name of their owners branded on their foreheads. There were a hundred bronze gates in the eleven miles of wall that ran around the city, and atop the walls were rooms large enough to hold four-horse chariots.

Nebuchadnezzar was determined to hold the southern half of the Assyrian domains that his father, Nabopolassar, had taken. When a city was not cooperative, Nebuchadnezzar seized its inhabitants—as he had the men of Jerusalem from their hilltop—marched them to Babylon with all the goods from their ruined temples, and put them to work as slaves. One building project, called the Hanging Gardens by the Greeks, had a garden placed over a vaulted substructure to look like a hill, a gift for Nebuchadnezzar's Median wife. Another was the long wall between the Tigris and Euphrates rivers, dubbed the Median wall, for the Babylonians had begun to suspect that their allies the Medes might one day grow strong enough to turn against them.

In 566 B.C., shortly after Cyrus had become king of the Persians, Nabonidus took over the kingship of Babylon. Both of his predecessors, who had succeeded Nebuchadnezzar, had brief and ineffectual reigns. Nabonidus did what he could in the midst of the fever and famine that beset Babylon during his rule, and he marched north to bring back thousands of new slaves. But through a series of miscalculations and blunders, he incited the anger of the city's more powerful inhabitants. He was an Aramaean, and while attempting to establish the Aramaean moon god, Sin, in Babylon, he reduced the royal allowance to the priests of the chief Babylonian god Bel-Marduk. Then, he left his unpopular son Belshazzar in charge of the city and went off to the Arabian desert to seize the city of Tema and make it a base from which to control the trade route to Egypt. He lost many warriors and many noblemen in the process. He seldom returned to Babylon for the important New Year's Day celebrations. He failed to drain the gulf, which was silting so badly that ships could not reach the tiled quays on the lower Tigris and Euphrates; nor did he fence property as was customary. To make amends, he finally threw a huge New Year's feast, but it was too late to quell the growing hostility of the priests, nobles, merchants, and landholders.

Cyrus, on the other hand, knew the value of friendship. He sent emissaries to establish contact with the discontented in Babylon in preparation for his plan to take the greatest city in the world. In 539 B.C., his soldiers dug up a tributary of the Tigris so that the Persian forces could ford its dispersed channels and enter Babylonia south of the Median wall. A Babylonian governor named Gobryas had pledged

his allegiance to Cyrus, and it was he who led the Persians to victory against the Babylonians at Opis that fall. Shortly afterward, Gobryas led the Persians into the city of Babylon itself. Again, the takeover was swift and bloodless. Well-behaved Persian soldiers hurried to the temple Esagila to guard it. Nabonidus returned and was quietly arrested. The people spread barley branches on the streets and turned out in throngs to watch the entry of the great conqueror

*"Very splendid did it turn out," Darius said of the palace with its Babylonian-style glazed brick friezes he built in Susa. The fifth century B.C. archers of the royal guard (preceding pages) and griffin (facing page) are typical Babylonian work. The man-bull and the humanized sacred palm tree (above) are far older, coming from a relief in one of the Elamite sanctuaries in Susa.*

# By the waters of Babylon

Wandering across the semidesert border-lands of Mesopotamia and Syria, a cluster of Semitic herding clans led by a patriarch named Abraham settled in the hills of Canaan near the Mediterranean sometime in the early part of the second millennium B.C. Some generations later, they moved south into Egypt during a famine; when a new ruler came to power, they were made slaves there, constructing palaces for the pharaohs. Moses led them to freedom, back to Canaan through the Sinai, and gave them laws. By about 1000 B.C., the Hebrews were settled as a confederation of tribes in Israel and Judea. The nearby Aramaeans, the distant Egyptians, and eventually the Assyrians exacted tribute from the Hebrews, and then in various campaigns the Assyrians and the Babylonians destroyed their cities and dragged the occupants off into exile.

Yet even in exile the Hebrew community maintained its integrity and never relinquished its hopes of returning to Palestine. "By the waters of Babylon, there we sat down and wept, when we remembered Zion" reads Psalm 137. It was not until Cyrus conquered Babylon in 538 B.C. that the Hebrews were freed and allowed to return to the promised land.

Left, the remains of the major Philistine city of Ashdod. Though the Hebrews had considerable friction with the Philistines, the two nations sometimes cooperated. When they did so in 710 B.C. to rebel against Assyrian rule, they were thoroughly smashed. Sargon II dictated: "I marched quickly—in my state chariot and with my cavalry which never, even if friendly territory, leaves my side—against Ashdod, his [Ashdod's ruler's] residence, and I besieged and conquered. . . . I declared the gods residing therein, himself, as well as the inhabitants of his country, the gold, silver, and his personal possessions as booty. I reorganized . . . and placed an officer of mine as governor over them and declared them Assyrian citizens, and they bore my yoke."

Inhabited from the fifth millennium B.C., Megiddo controlled the main pass through the Carmel range. As a terraced and prosperous Canaanite town, Megiddo was frequently attacked. The Hebrews conquered it in the twelfth century, and King Solomon, who ruled for about forty years in the mid-tenth century B.C., built a sturdy wall (whose ruins appear at top). The Assyrians were next to take Megiddo, followed by the Babylonians.

Hebrews who fought for their cities ran the risk of being deported to the lands of the conquerors. Hebrew captives from the ancient fortified city of Lachish west of Hebron in Palestine (immediately above) guide a laden camel from the Judean hills to the Mesopotamian plain.

Because the history of the Hebrew people is recorded in the central book of Western civilization, we are familiar with the sorrows of their slavery. The painful captivity in Egypt was not too different from that in Assyria: inhabitants of defeated towns were marched off with carts (top) to labor hauling stones and wood for a palace (immediately above), and were taught to raise their hands in surrender and supplication (left). These reliefs showing the captives of Lachish are from Sennacherib's palace.

*Below, the ruins of Babylon. Built on the banks of the Euphrates, Babylon was relatively unimportant until the Semites took over the Sumerian cities. Then, as Hammurabi's royal capital in the eighteenth century B.C., Babylon became the most imposing sight on the Mesopotamian plain and long remained so. As Akkad itself declined in power, the Hittites took Babylon, then the Kassites, then the Elamites, and finally the Assyrians. Much of what archaeologists have unearthed on the site dates from later times, after the independent king Nebuchadnezzar restored Babylon in the sixth century B.C. Under him, the great city flourished once again.*

*Right, the ruins of Nebuchadnezzar's palace in Babylon. A prodigious builder, Nebuchadnezzar had a hanging garden created for his Median wife who missed the hills; it was considered one of the Seven Wonders of the World in Hellenistic times. It was in this palace, according to the Book of Daniel, that king Belshazzar, the grandson of Nebuchadnezzar, held the great and voluptuous feast interrupted by the strange writing on the wall prophesying the downfall of Babylon.*

from the East, whom they welcomed as a savior.

"He is my shepherd," the Hebrew god said of Cyrus, according to the prophecy of Second Isaiah, "whose right hand I have holden, to subdue nations before him . . . yea, I have called him; I have brought him." Cyrus himself announced that Bel-Marduk had called him and led him into Babylon. After the king of kings sacrificed to Marduk, the lord of lords, he had the Babylonian statues, too long ignored, washed. He then offered sacrifices, as had been the custom until Nabonidus depleted the funds of the priesthood. Cyrus ordered the other idols—which Nabonidus had hurriedly brought into the city from surrounding towns that summer in hopes that their power would help save Babylon—to be carried home. And Cyrus freed earlier captives, gave them their wooden gods and their temple goods, and sent them home to rebuild their own temples. He thus assured himself of loyal allies, including thousands of Jerusalemites, who saw Cyrus as their liberator and the anointed of the Lord. "Sing, O ye heaven; for the Lord has done it," sang the Jews who left their exile in Babylon with even greater faith in the one God: "I, even I, am the Lord. . . . I am the first and I am the last; and beside me there is no God."

Cyrus picked up a basket full of earth to carry on

his head, a traditional signal to repair the city. Babylon was to be his administrative capital. Phoenician ambassadors arrived to kiss his feet and put at his disposal the best fleet in the world. The Arabs, whom Nabonidus had subdued, flocked to the city, bringing a thousand pounds of frankincense as the first part of their tribute. Cyrus set an annual tribute for Babylon that was probably on the order of a later rate of 66,000 pounds or 1,000 talents of silver and 500 castrated boys. "I am Cyrus," he proclaimed without qualm, "king of the world."

But before Babylon came Lydia. There, the rich king Croesus reacted slowly to Cyrus's takeover of Ecbatana in 550 B.C. Finally, in the spring of 547 B.C., he crossed the boundary at the Halys River and seized the old Median fort at Pteria in Cappadocia. When the news reached Cyrus at his summer palace at Ecbatana, he immediately prepared his army for the long march to the Mesopotamian plain.

The baggage went first, loaded onto camels and an assortment of pack animals. Then came the cavalry on small horses whose bridles were tied with beads and bells. One thousand foot soldiers in Elamite, Babylonian, eastern Iranian, Scythian, Persian, and Median dress followed the cavalrymen. A special wagon carried the silver altar and the sacred Aryan fire. Cyrus rode in a golden chariot followed by thousands of footmen and horsemen. Cooks, repairmen, and slaves brought up the rear.

Ashur and several other Assyrian cities fell to Cyrus on his march to confront the Lydians. Prudently, he organized the conquered cities into a province with local administrators who pledged loyalty to Cyrus. Then he marched north to the mountains, securing Armenia and assessing a tribute of thousands of colts per year. Finally, the army reached Cappadocia. Along the way, Cyrus had been sending emissaries ahead to sound out the cities farther west. He was particularly interested in the Greek cities of Ionia at the western tip of the Anatolian peninsula, past Lydia. These were not only rich trading centers but also the home of the best fleet on the Mediterranean, next to the Phoenicians. Of these cities, only the greatest, Miletus, showed any interest in joining Cyrus in war against Croesus. The other cities would pay for their lack of enthusiasm.

Cyrus reached the fort at Pteria. For a day, the Persian foot soldiers and cavalrymen fought the Lydian lancers to a stand-off. Croesus had been told by the Greek oracle at Delphi, "If you cross the Halys, you will destroy an empire," and he confidently as-

*The Persians were so struck by the walls of Babylon that they reproduced the Babylonian designs in the palace at Susa. The north wall of Babylon was pierced by the gates of Ishtar, the goddess of love and war, and decorated with bulls symbolizing Adad, the god of lightning, and dragon-snakes symbolizing Marduk, the chief Babylonian god. Lions represented the goddess Ishtar, and from the temple of Marduk to a smaller temple by the Euphrates stretched the spectacular Processional Way, lined on either side with 120 lions in enameled bricks (below). The lions were molded in relief, cut into bricks, glazed with colored enamel, and reassembled.*

sumed that the destroyed empire would be Persia. But Croesus withdrew. He headed for his fortress city of Sardes and paid his mercenaries in the gold coin for which he was famous. It was now autumn, and nobody fought during the cold months. By spring, he probably reasoned, some of his Ionian, Egyptian, or Spartan allies would come to his aid.

But Cyrus came after him and, employing a tactic suggested by his general Harpagus, put the pack camels in the front line. When the horses in Croesus's rear guard smelled the dreaded camels, they bolted. Nevertheless, most of the Lydian soldiers were already safely stationed behind the walls of Sardes. By

following a Lydian soldier who had gone outside the walls to retrieve a fallen helmet, the Persians stole into the city and unleashed upon it the anger and destruction they had spared those cities that had willingly capitulated.

Word of surrender began to come in quickly from all over Anatolia. Cyrus sent his soldiers to seize all the Greek cities but Miletus, which was allowed simply to open its gates. Fearing slavery, the Greek inhabitants of the Lydian town of Phocaea packed themselves into galleys and took to sea. Others followed suit. Few cities could hope to withstand the Persian army, whose reputation was now universally feared. There were armored horsemen, thousands strong, well trained in the use of the spear and the javelin. There were helmeted charioteers, who drove chariots fitted with whirring blades sharp as scythes. And there were the foot soldiers. Wearing quilted linen armor or coats of bronze or gold, they carried rectangular wicker shields, arrows tipped with bronze or iron, or seven-foot spears. When these weapons failed, the men could resort to using short swords, knives, and slings. The Persian army was a war machine designed to win by sheer force of numbers. And it always did.

The Greek cities in Asia were broken. Some Greeks were taken into the Persian army as mercenaries; others were sold into slavery. Phrygia was taken by force and Cilicia capitulated.

The Ionian cities that looked onto the Aegean were especially important, for Cyrus and for history. They were the site of many modern developments. Here, a new kind of thought flourished—practical, secular, scientific. In the midst of violence and turmoil came the beginnings of philosophy. The ancient gods had been abandoned. Heraclitus of Ephesus said that everything flows and changes, nothing is fixed or eternal. Thales of Miletus had been to Egypt and had used Egypt's land-measuring geometry at sea on his return voyage. He also introduced to the Greeks the Egyptians' efficient 365-day year. Thales had even predicted the eclipse of 585 B.C., which had brought on the truce between the Medes and Lydians. Anaximander of Miletus had drawn a map of the world for his town's merchant seamen, who sent ships to Egypt, to the western Mediterranean, and into the Black Sea. He did not believe that any god had made the world but said rather that four elements had pre-existed the creation; when the fire from the sun penetrated through the mist (not quite the same as our idea of air), it evaporated some of the water and revealed the dry land. He reasoned that the first men

had descended from marine creatures who came onto the land when the seas dried. His townsman Anaximenes said that fire, water, and earth were simply rarefied or condensed versions of mist, which was matter in its original form.

The Ionians had abandoned their kings along with many old ideas and had less than the usual respect for landowners. They were ruled by tyrants, powerful merchants who were understandably happy to have the vast market of the Persian Empire opened to them. The Greek cities of the nearby islands surrendered without a fight, and the fleet of the Greeks was now at the disposal of Cyrus. With Greek and Phoe-

nician triremes, it would now be possible to invade Egypt. But Cyrus had been called away to the eastern border of the Iranian plateau by the time his generals completed the conquest of the Anatolian peninsula.

Between his Lydian and Babylonian campaigns, Cyrus, now in his thirties, crossed the Iranian plateau to subdue the nomadic people of the East. Beyond the northeast edge of the plateau were sandy plains, a windy desert, and the Oxus River. Cyrus crossed the Oxus on inflated animal skins and claimed the rocky gorges and hills of Sogdiana and its capital, Maracanda (which would become Samarkand). Farther east at the Jaxartes River, he stopped. Beyond it were

## "I Cyrus, king, Achaemenid"

Pasargadae, meaning "camp of the Persians," is where the herders of Persis established a small village in the bend of the Karum River. It is on this site that Cyrus the Great is said to have defeated his grandfather Astyages to become king of kings. When Cyrus had the wealth to build, he planned a complex of palaces, temples, and gardens here as his royal residence that would cover a mile and a half of nearby land. He had huge blocks of stone set into a terrace to overlook the high plateau and ordered a modest stone mausoleum built for himself. It was set among trees, pavilions, and water channels. Cyrus did not live to see the palace; when it was built, it was basically Median or Urartian in style, with white limestone over mud walls and black limestone for door and window frames. On the terrace was a tower which may have been designed to hold the sacred fire. When Cyrus's body was brought back after his death in the East, it was dressed in golden garments and laid in the tomb. Several Magi made monthly sacrifices of a horse for Cyrus, in return for which they received flour and a whole sheep each day. A common inscription on various plaques at Pasargadae (above) reads, in Old Persian, Elamite, and Babylonian, "I, Cyrus, king, Achaemenid, [built this]."

the grasslands inhabited by a wild Scythian group, the Massagetae. On the river bank Cyrus built seven forts to mark the northeastern boundary of his conquest. He then pushed southeastward to the fertile Bactrian plain and onward to Sattagyida and Gandhara, where the mountains, rich in minerals, drop to the Indus valley. By now Cyrus had doubled the size of Iranian territory and taken thousands of horses in tribute, which he would later use against Babylon.

Cyrus had to put aside his long-calculated plans to enter Egypt when he was called back to his eastern frontier by trouble near the Jaxartes in 530 B.C. In a violent battle with the Scythian queen Tomyris, Cyrus was killed. The father of the Persian people was carried home to the tomb he had built for himself at Pasargadae, where he had begun to raise a grand ceremonial city built on a vast terrace made up of blocks of stone. A modest stone mausoleum was waiting for him, set in a paradise of gardens planted with every species of tree in the empire. His successors would complete both Pasargadae and the conquest of the Egyptian Empire.

Word of the death of Cyrus reached his son Cambyses II in Babylon during the summer of 530 B.C. The new king soon took up his father's plan to invade Egypt. He set out across the Arabian desert for the Sinai. The Arabs had promised his army safe conduct and had placed jugs of water along a notoriously dry strip. The shield-hung ships of Ionia and Phoenicia would be waiting for Cambyses at Pelusium, at the mouth of the Nile. So would Egypt's pharaoh, Psamtik III, with an army.

Cambyses won the ensuing battle and followed the fleeing Egyptians south to Memphis, which he put to siege and took in 525 B.C. The Libyans soon surrendered, and their cities of Cyrene and Barca sent gifts in a gesture of peace. Cambyses designated the entire empire of Egypt as a single province, or satrapy, which would be taxed eventually at 120,000 loads of grain and 46,000 pounds of silver. He planned three new campaigns to extend Persian domination to the limits of the known world. Then his luck changed.

Cambyses wanted to sail west past Cyrene to Carthage, perhaps even to the end of the Mediterranean, but the Phoenicians refused to make war on Carthage, their own colony. An army sent against the Oasis of Amon failed in the midst of a sandstorm. Finally Cambyses himself led an expedition into Ethiopia. Foolishly, he headed south along the infertile banks of the upper Nile without sufficient food. As a result, the Persian soldiers were forced to eat their pack animals. They kept on, fighting over what little food they found. Eventually, they had nothing to eat but each other, and Cambyses had no choice but to

*Cyrus (facing page) proclaimed of himself and his greatest deed: "Marduk, the great lord, a protector of his worshipers, beheld with pleasure his [Cyrus's] good deeds and his upright heart and ordered him to march against his city Babylon. He made him set out on the road to Babylon, going at his side like a real friend. His widespread troops strolled along, their weapons packed away. Without any battle, he made him enter his town Babylon, sparing Babylon any calamity."*

turn back. The Persians had not failed entirely for, unlike any other conquerors, they succeeded in occupying all of Egypt.

The Egyptians and the Greeks claimed that Cambyses went mad on the return to Egypt. It is told that he kicked and killed a pregnant sister-wife and that he shot a friend's son to demonstrate his marksmanship, and there are stories of his excessive drinking and obsessive need to be reassured that he was a man to equal his father. On his way home, in 522 B.C., Cambyses heard that a pretender had seized the throne he had left in Babylon. It is said that he jumped from his horse, was accidentally stabbed in the thigh by his own sword, and died.

A young Achaemenid named Darius, who had been a young officer in Cyrus's last expedition and commander of Cambyses's elite troops in Egypt, was the one who brought the army home and eventually quelled the rebellion that was surfacing throughout the empire. Darius and six other noblemen killed the pretender to the throne in Babylon. Then Darius traveled to the remote capital Pasargadae and, in 522 B.C., put on the robe of Cyrus and ate the ancient ceremonial meal of figs and sour milk at his coronation. Only four of the now twenty-three satraps offered loyalty. Since rebellion was considered the worst

*From the ruins of Cyrus's palace at Pasargadae comes this fragment (left) of a fish god carved in bas-relief. Cyrus's nearby tomb (below) was built of white limestone atop a flight of stairs. Its double sloping roof is reminiscent of early wooden houses in Iran and of his ancestors' wooden tombs. Once set within a paradise of trees of every species, the tomb now rests on sand. A stone terrace (right), built by Cyrus, was called the "Throne of the Mother of Solomon."*

crime, earning the worst punishment, Darius ordered many crucifixions—three thousand in Babylon alone. It took him two years to restore order in the empire. Then, he put on the purple robe, took up his five-foot scepter, and ascended the lion-legged throne. It was time for peace.

Darius recognized that a more organized and powerful central government was essential, but it was not to be based on force: diplomacy would be a key to dealing with the many peoples and lands now drawn together. He sent Persian inspectors through the empire to evaluate the activities of local administrators and to assess how much each field and site of manufacture could produce per year. He taxed the satraps at about twenty percent of their nation's income. He also tightened satrapal management, giving local officials Persian counterparts to work with them. Many of these Persian administrators were members of the Seven Achaemenid Families (the seven families being those of the men who had killed the pretender, including that of Darius). A unit of the Persian army was settled in each satrapy to provide a check on the satrap's personal army. Darius also helped consolidate his kingdom by establishing a unified coinage and setting an exact rate of exchange between gold and silver.

# All that glitters

Gold, the king of metals, was well loved by the Persians, who were descendants of metalworking nomads obliged to carry their wealth on their bodies or in their wagons. Solid gold bracelets, armlets, earrings, chains, and breastplates were worn by upper-class men and women alike. For the table there were gold cups, pitchers, plates, and bowls—some bearing names or scenes from old traditional tales. There were sacred objects of gold, idols and their decorations as well as plaques, figurines, and toys. The Medes, Cimmerians, and Scythians were highly regarded for their gold work. Craftsmen in gold were sent on projects across the empire and were paid the early Achaemenid standard craft rate of one silver shekel a month, along with a pan of barley. Golden vessels were a form of capital and were essential to temple and palace. The writer of the Book of Esther would later recount that some of the beds at Shusan, the palace at Susa, were made of gold and that guests drank wine from a variety of golden cups, often decorated with realistically rendered animals.

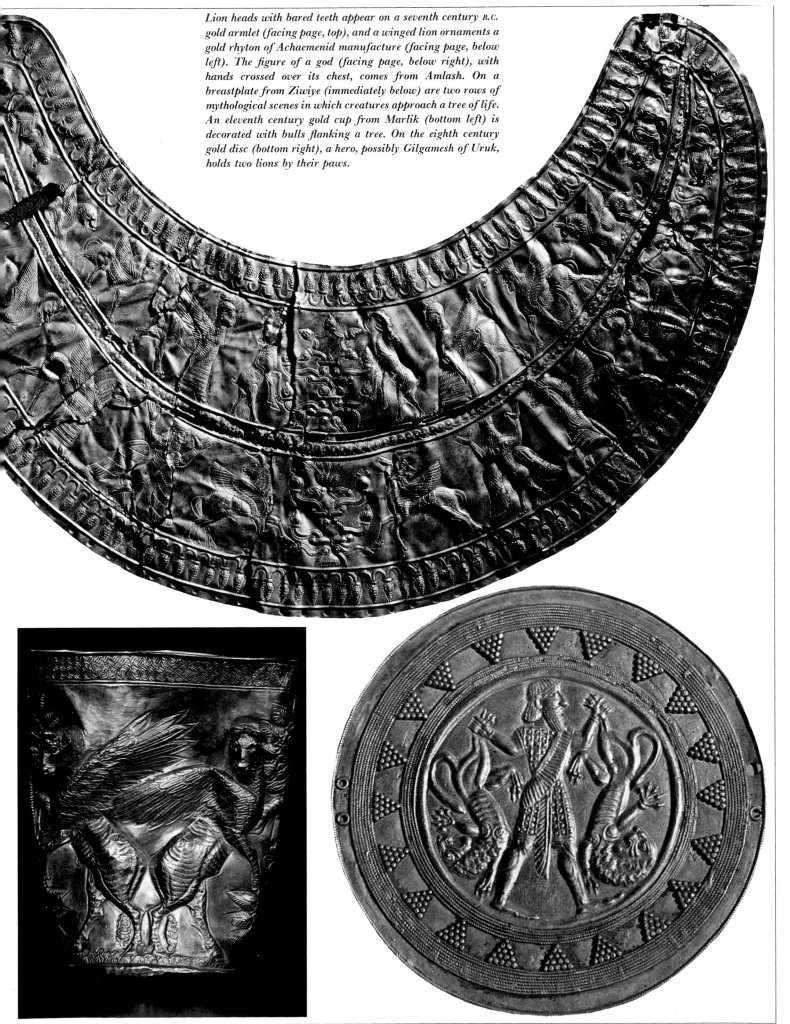

Lion heads with bared teeth appear on a seventh century B.C. gold armlet (facing page, top), and a winged lion ornaments a gold rhyton of Achaemenid manufacture (facing page, below left). The figure of a god (facing page, below right), with hands crossed over its chest, comes from Amlash. On a breastplate from Ziwiye (immediately below) are two rows of mythological scenes in which creatures approach a tree of life. An eleventh century gold cup from Marlik (bottom left) is decorated with bulls flanking a tree. On the eighth century gold disc (bottom right), a hero, possibly Gilgamesh of Uruk, holds two lions by their paws.

*Left, an Egyptian statue from the Persian period of a man holding an image of a god in a tiny tabernacle. The map (below) shows the itinerary of Cambyses's Egyptian campaign: Joined by Ionian Greeks at Gaza, he crossed the Sinai desert with the help of the Bedouins to the Pelusiac branch of the Nile, where the first fighting occurred. After taking Memphis and imprisoning the pharaoh, Cambyses staged three notably unsuccessful campaigns: against Carthage, the Oasis of Amon, and Ethiopia.*

Slaves and rebels were sent to Susa in Elam, still in ruins, where they were employed to build a great palace. The Babylonians did the brick glazing, the Ionians and Lydians cut the stone, and the Medes and Egyptians worked the gold. Susa became a new Babylon, and here the king received reports of legal cases monitored in the satrapies and news from his inspectors and overseers.

When he was at the palace in Susa, only a privileged few were allowed in the presence of the great king as he sat at his meals, often behind a veil draped across an archway. The members of the Seven Families were required only to bend a knee in his presence, while all others were to prostrate themselves. In the summer, the court moved to the palace at Ecbatana to avoid the extreme heat at Susa.

Darius decided to build a higher, cooler palace city in Persis. The Greeks would call it Persepolis. Darius chose the site and began the rock terrace of Persepolis fifty feet above the Iranian plateau. He built the monumental staircase where the emissaries of all the satrapies and vassal states would carry the symbols of their tribute each New Year's Day, and he decorated it with stone reliefs representing each of these subject peoples.

With the empire in order, Darius turned to expansion. Gandhara in the southeast made a good starting

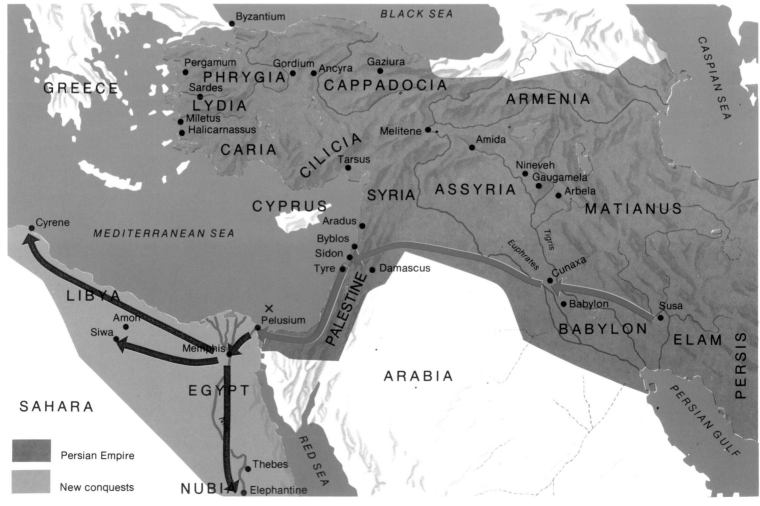

Persian Empire

New conquests

point for his soldiers, who secured the land rich in pearls, tortoiseshell, and spices that lay between Bactria and India. The Indian tax was to be the highest in the empire: 360 talents of gold. To explore the seas of the empire, Darius had an Ionian sailor named Scylax command a fleet which sailed down the Indus, into the Indian Ocean, and west around Sinai to Egypt. When Scylax arrived at Suez on the Red Sea about thirty months later, Darius conceived a plan to go straight through to the Mediterranean.

About a hundred years earlier, the pharaoh Necho had tried unsuccessfully to dig a canal from the Red Sea to the Nile. Darius set his engineers to pry out a watercourse 150 feet wide and 90 miles long, from Suez north to the Pelusiac branch of the Nile. Ships then could load their pearls on the Indus docks and unload on the wharves in Ionia. Returning, ships could pick up Phoenician cedar, Egyptian glass, and Ethiopian ivory and unload this invaluable cargo on

*Below, the cliffs of Egypt seen from the Red Sea. A desert stretches miles inland beyond these cliffs toward the distant cultivated strip along the Nile. After his unsuccessful expedition into Ethiopia, Cambyses led his forces across the desert with great difficulty, having hoped to speed his return to Memphis.*

the tiled quays of the Tigris and Euphrates.

Though the southern ocean was Persia's, the Mediterranean still belonged, in large part, to the Greeks. Before attacking the Greeks head on, Darius decided to secure the parts of Europe closest to him on his northwestern borders: the Scythian steppes north of the Black Sea and the grain and timberlands of Thrace just beyond the Bosporus and the Hellespont. The cooperation of Thrace would be needed for all subsequent crossings from Asia to Europe.

At the suggestion of an Ionian engineer, Darius had hundreds of Ionian ships bound together over the three-quarter-mile width of the Hellespont. Across them was stretched a long ramp which had solid walls so that animals crossing would not shy as they passed over it. Thousands of horses and seventy thousand soldiers crossed the bridge, rested, and marched for the Danube, where engineers built another bridge and the army crossed into the steppes. Here, Darius sought the Scythians day after day, but the horsemen were already in their mobile wagons, retreating from him. As the Scythians backed off, they burned the summer grasses behind them and filled the wells with salt. Lured farther and farther from the coast of the Black Sea where ships waited to supply him, Darius finally sent off an impatient message urging the

Scythians to stand and fight. Their reply was succinct: "Go weep."

Exhausted, starved, and beaten by these evasive tactics, the enormous army of the Persian Empire fell back to the pontoon bridge at the Hellespont just in time. The Ionian shipmasters had decided that Darius was not returning and were about to disengage and return home. A small Persian force stayed behind to secure Thrace, which eventually submitted. The door to Europe had been opened, but just barely.

Soon after, in 499 B.C., the city of Miletus led the other Ionian cities in a revolt. They received aid from Athens and Eretria on the Greek mainland, but even with such help the Ionians could not take their target, Sardes. So they burned it. In return, Darius seized Miletus, destroyed its temples, and sent its people to Susa as captives. Then Darius sent envoys to the Greek cities to determine which were ready to capitulate. All were humbled, except Athens, Sparta, and Eretria.

Darius smashed Eretria in six days; it was never rebuilt. In 490 B.C., he moved a fleet of predominantly Phoenician ships in near Marathon on the Greek mainland. The soldiers aboard the ships made camp on land and prepared to march on Athens at dawn. But in the famous battle of Marathon, the Athenian

In this limestone relief (above) from the Hall of Audience at Persepolis, an emissary from greater Persia is being led to the king. Darius sits enthroned, his feet on a stool. Behind him stands Xerxes, the crown prince. Both are rendered larger than all other figures, a tradition for royalty in both Mesopotamia and Egypt. And both wear the square-tipped royal beard. Twin censors separate the Great King from his vassal.

High above the old caravan route to Babylon at Behistun, in western Iran, the official biography of Darius (right) was carved into sheer rock: to be certain no vandal would deface the eight-by-ten-foot panel, Darius had the steps used by the artisans obliterated and the rock cut smooth directly below the relief. Darius, shown with his foot on the prostrate Gaumata and with other rebels safely roped, reports: "When Cambyses had gone to Egypt . . . Gaumata lied to the people thus: 'I am Bardiya, the son of Cyrus, brother of Cambyses.' . . . I with a few men slew that Gaumata the Magian and those chief men who were his supporters. . . . Ahura Mazda bestowed the kingdom upon me."

*Preceding pages, a view of Persepolis, the capital designed by Darius the Great about thirty miles southwest of Pasargadae. In the background are the Zagros; at center is the Hall of a Hundred Columns built by Darius's son Xerxes; behind that is Darius's Hall of Audience, of which thirteen stone columns remain, where he watched the annual procession of tributaries. Southward (at rear left) are the palaces of Darius, Xerxes, and Artaxerxes III. In the left foreground and in detail (this page, left) are the remains of the treasury.*

*Above, the main gateway on the south side of the gold-paneled palace where Darius washed, dressed, and dined when he was at Persepolis for festivities. The door and window frames were carved out of single pieces of stone. The building of the Persepolis structures and the great terrace made of stone blocks on which they stand supplied employment for over a sixty-year period, from approximately 520 to 460 B.C. Persepolis was neither a diplomatic nor an administrative center; it was instead conceived by Darius as the ceremonial symbol of imperial unity.*

infantry charged the Persian bowmen and spearmen, chased them back to their ships, and even pulled their anchor cables out of the water. The Persians spent the night aboard ship and sailed the next day into the harbor at Athens, determined to take the city from the sea instead. But beset by the tireless Athenian infantry, Darius took a loss of thousands of men and many ships. The doorway of Thrace, as it turned out, was all that Persia would ever hold in Europe. Darius went home, where he died in 486 B.C. He was buried in a tomb cut into a rock cliff near Persepolis.

Xerxes, the second-born son of Darius, inherited most of the world and wanted the rest: "I shall pass through Europe from end to end and make it all one country." First, he brutally crushed revolts in Egypt and Babylon, destroying Babylon's temple, Esagila, and melting down the golden statue of Bel-Marduk. Then he turned toward Greece, ordering two boat bridges built across the Hellespont. When a storm arose and destroyed them, Xerxes had the disobedient sea lashed three hundred times, more lashes than any man could survive. His histrionics were well recorded by contemporary chroniclers.

In the spring of 480 B.C., the forty-year-old Xerxes built another pair of bridges. This time, he poured a libation of wine into the water and prayed to Mithra,

The animal-headed columns of the Persians are perhaps their most distinctive gift to architecture. The griffin (above), the lion (immediately below), and the bull (bottom) were designed as halves of back-to-back twin heads as much as eight feet wide for the tops of sixty-five-foot-high columns. There were seventy-two such columns in the Hall of Audience. An Assyrian-style human-headed, winged, bearded, and hatted bull (left) is one of a pair standing wary guard at the gate of Xerxes.

god of light and guardian against evil; he tossed in the gold cup too, and the great crossing began. One bridge was strewn with myrtle boughs and scented with perfume. Wearing garlands, the elite cavalry troops, called the Ten Thousand Immortals, crossed first. The king's chariot followed on the next day. On the other bridge, attendants, slaves, and baggage-bearing animals made their slow, lash-encouraged progress. The Aegean was filled to the horizon with more than a thousand ships from Egypt, Phoenicia, and the Greek cities of Asia. Each ship was manned by thirty sailors, mostly Persians, Medes, or Scythians. There were perhaps two million fighting men of

forty-six nationalities, led by twenty-nine Persian generals. Among them were Cissians in turbans, Assyrians with bronze helmets, Bactrians with cane bows, Scythians with battle-axes, Indians in cotton, Caspians in leather, Arabs in belted robes, Ethiopians wearing leopard skins and smeared red and white for battle, Paphlagonians with wicker helmets, and Cappadocians in high boots. Most were mercenaries with little interest in glorifying Persia. There were eighty thousand horses, many in heavy chain armor that

*On the eastern ceremonial stairway to the Hall of Audience at Persepolis, the lion of summer bites the bull of winter (left and below left). The Persian imperial guards known as the Ten Thousand Immortals (below) stand in relief on the stairway where actual guards would pose while the king and his nobles passed by. The 111 steps of the stairway were fifty feet wide with four-inch risers, enabling ten horses—pulling chariots—to mount them abreast.*

would encumber them in war. At the end of the enormous army came women, eunuchs, and dogs.

Xerxes was confident that no Greek soldier would dare oppose him. He reached Thermopylae in August and gave the Spartans—whom his spies found combing out their hair for battle—a few days to reconsider and retreat. Instead, they stood heroically against him. With considerable effort, the great king finally crushed Leonidas's army, killing every last man. Only then could he make his way to Athens, where he burned the Acropolis. Relieved, he joined his fleet at Salamis, which was reduced by storms. There he suffered his worst defeat, losing thousands of men and much of his fleet. He barely made it back to the Hellespont in October, only to find his bridges destroyed by storms. He had his men ferried home and this time did not stop to lash the waters. For the next fifteen years, Xerxes glorified Persepolis and superintended his increasingly luxurious court. But Persia had been depopulated by the wars and lived in fear of the king's whim.

At its height, the Persian Empire was as rich and varied in culture as it was in extent. The Achaemenids invited doctors from the Ionian island of Cos to treat their illnesses. Greek scientists and philosophers traveled to Babylon and Egypt to query and be queried. Phoenician explorers were interviewed at court, and literary men and historians were welcomed there. Wherever the bureaucracy operated, the army garrisons settled with their families, or the merchant corps traveled, a single ecumenical culture grew out of the diversity.

The Persians prided themselves on being humane and just rulers and earned a reputation for tolerance that makes the lapses into violence the exception rather than the rule. Conquered peoples were treated with respect by Cyrus and Darius and allowed to maintain their way of life to a large extent unchanged. Persian law developed out of tribal law and from ancient Mesopotamian precedents. The Sumerian codes had been translated into Akkadian and later rewritten under Darius. He took full credit for this impressive Aramaean ordinance. Unfortunately, scholars know little about these regulations because they were recorded on papyrus, which long ago turned to dust.

The laws of the Persians were immutable. When Xerxes's wife, Esther, begged him to remand his edict for the killing of the Jews, he could not retract the decree. His only recourse was to send out a directive urging the Jews to defend themselves. Persian punishments were also harsh. A defendant found to have lied in court could be mutilated, impaled, banished, or even crucified, while a corrupt judge could be flayed and the judicial chair covered with his skin as a warning to future judges tempted by bribes. The common man probably felt relieved at being protected from the whims of his superiors by the law, but not so much so that he could lose his fear of running afoul of it. Nations that had not yet written down their codes, or even invented them, were guided by many of the precedents set by the Persians.

The sixth century B.C. is noted for the founding of three of the world's major religious or philosophical systems: ethical Confucianism; introspective Buddhism; and Persia's dualistic Zoroastrianism. Zoroaster, or Zarathustra, was probably a Mede born in 628 B.C. in the northeast of the Iranian plateau. He helped elevate one of the "good forces," or *ahuras,* of the Aryan pantheon to be a supreme god. This force, Ahura Mazda, was like time—eternal and unchanging. He was invisible, and he created all things, spiritual and material. The only force that equaled him was an evil one called Ahriman—darkness, death, the changing time that corrupts, the lie.

*An inscription in cuneiform bears the name of Xerxes, at the entrance to a tomb in Anatolia (top), where the upper classes tended to adopt Persian art forms. When Xerxes built at Persepolis, he had this drainage canal (immediately above) put into the courtyard outside his palace. Once he ascended the throne, Xerxes was embarrassed by the reliefs of himself as crown prince on the walls of the Hall of Audience so he built the Hall of a Hundred Columns. A relief from the hall (near right) shows Xerxes enthroned above ranks of Persian and Median guards.*

Xerxes's palace, which contained the window frame above, adjoined a harem in which untried women prepared themselves for weeks or even months for their single night with the king—after which they could be moved either to concubine or, more rarely, wifely quarters to further attend the king. The king spent most of his time with the men of the Seven (Achaemenid) Families, who drank, wore false hair, and used cosmetics. Below, a fifth century gold cup bearing Xerxes's name around its rim, incised trilingually in cuneiform.

# Who was who in Persian society?

The social structure of the Achaemenid Empire was based upon land, and theoretically, the king owned it all. The top nobles were those of the Achaemenid Seven Families, from which came satraps, army officers, the king's bodyguard, and his wives, managers, and overseers. Priests also exercised some power. Subject peoples paid all the taxes, while all male Persians originally were required to give military service; after Cyrus a professional army was established. Veterans were rewarded with land and formed a class of small landowners. Artisans migrated to large construction projects. Freemen or serfs who came with the land barely scraped by. Servants and slaves generally received better treatment, as they represented investments which had to be protected, but they were often mutilated to prevent them from running away. Slaves were persons before the law and could own property, even other slaves. Women could work as tavern keepers, wine sellers, and artisans.

*Fashioned in lapis lazuli paste, this Achaemenid prince (above), possibly a young Xerxes, was found at Persepolis and wears a crown on which the battlements resemble those of the capital. A satrap was next in glory to the Achaemenid royalty and often came, during the later days of the empire, from among the Seven Families. Above right, a satrap seated on his throne, from mid-fifth century Phoenicia.*

*Right, the image of the great god Ahura Mazda. The god's wings indicated the sky, from where Ahura Mazda reigned, and enfolded the earth and its just ruler, who ruled on the god's behalf. The wings of the god, above which rises its torso, may have been derived from the wings of the Egyptian sky god Horus.*

The sweet life was available to precious few in Achaemenid times. Left, a silver statuette of a dignitary sporting a traveling outfit, probably from the time of Artaxerxes II. Above, members of the king's personal guard parade; they are probably from the Seven Families. Iranian dignitaries press hands upon each other's chests (right), an expression of trust. It was a gentlemen's world: wives rarely saw men, even their brothers.

Backstairs and outdoors, the Persian lower classes labored. A peasant carries a sack of foodstuffs on his shoulder (near right). It probably weighed a talent, an ancient measurement from an early Mesopotamian word meaning "burden." The talent may have represented the weight a man could carry comfortably on a day's journey—about sixty-six pounds. Bearing a towel and other necessities for the king's bath (far right), a servant walks with a set smile. Although a servant had some rights before the law, insolence to his master was not among them. Both bas-reliefs are from Darius's palace.

# Nation of nations

Although Darius and his court lived mainly at Susa and Ecbatana, it was to Persepolis that the Great King came each year on New Year's Day, at the beginning of spring, to inaugurate the magnificent ceremonies consecrating the unity of the empire.

Under the aegis of the great god Ahura Mazda and in the presence of the king of kings, the master peoples (Persians and Medes) witnessed a procession of representatives of all the subject nations who had come to place gifts and offerings at the foot of the throne as tokens of loyalty. Following the carefully conceived design of Darius, all the edifices on the terrace of Persepolis were built, arranged, and adorned with reliefs in accordance with the role each was to play in the New Year's ceremony, the whole conveying a sense of power, stability, and grandeur. The long lines of subjects bearing tribute carved in relief on the stairways impress a visitor with both the power of the ruler and the variety of peoples—and products—to be found throughout the empire.

Though the resources and talents of conquered nations were exploited during both war and peace, the Achaemenids in general ruled with a light hand, unless local populations threatened rebellion. In many areas the actual presence of Persian domination was hardly noticeable. The Persians respected the cultural characteristics of each people, and even themselves adopted the dress of the Medes, the coinage of the Lydians, and the foods of the Greeks.

*The numerous peoples subject to the Great King, with the exception of the Persians, were obligated to send valuable tribute each year. Tribute-bearers (top, left to right) include a Median warrior; a skirted Indian carrying baskets; three Cappadocians bringing woven coats and trousers; and two Babylonians with tasseled hats guiding a humped zebu. Center, left to right, a Phrygian subject; a Lydian balancing two vases; Bactrians waiting to be presented by a Persian; and Chorasmians bringing fabrics. Bottom, left to right, Scythians escorting a horse and carrying armlets; an Armenian following with a vase; and Assyrians delivering rams.*

Such a dualistic view had been developing slowly; Zoroaster's contribution was to make it explicit. Each man, he taught, must choose his path and fight daily for the right in order to escape eternal damnation and reach everlasting life. Zoroaster's *Gathas,* or hymns, found him no followers until he had reached middle age, and those were in the conservative east of the Iranian plateau. Cyrus sacrificed to Anahita, goddess of water and fertility, as well as to Ahura Mazda. But Zoroaster's influence eventually spread through the empire. Darius was careful to show the great god hovering above him in portrait reliefs. Xerxes also supported Ahura Mazda as the one god, but his suc-

cessor, Artaxerxes, was quick to return Mithra and Anahita to importance.

Throughout the empire, religion was changing. The old astral gods of the nomads were blending with the earth gods of the farming population. The Jews were beginning to unite their monotheism with Egypt's ideas of judgment and resurrection (first mentioned in the Book of Daniel) and with Iran's evil power, or devil. Theirs was a system that would survive to our own day and, after further mixture with Greek doctrine, prepare the way for Christianity.

In finance, Darius set up a standardized, flexible system of coinage. Though Croesus of Lydia pro-

*Carved into the mountain side overlooking Persepolis, the 74-foot-high tomb of Artaxerxes III (facing page) is built on the model followed by all the Achaemenid kings, a style which can be traced to the Medes. As in the tombs of the great kings at Naqsh-i-Rustam (see pages 78–80), the four-columned façade was meant to resemble that of a palace, while the frieze above the columns and a written inscription connected the king's deeds with the god Ahura Mazda.*

*Also overlooking Persepolis is the tomb of Artaxerxes II (left), which bears the traditional carvings in the frieze above the tomb door: the king stands with his bow on a dais, worshiping the sacred fire. Below the king are his subject peoples and above is the winged symbol of Ahura Mazda. At first the god was shown as a winged disc, but his symbol gradually grew more complicated, incorporating features used to portray Assyrian and Egyptian deities.*

# To the sea in ships

The Phoenicians were the first people who took to the sea. A Semitic-speaking Canaanite people, they lived along the eastern coast of the Mediterranean, occupying most of modern Lebanon and areas to the south. In the third millennium B.C., these hearty sailors linked the river cultures of Mesopotamia and Egypt. From their own stands of hardwoods—the Biblical cedars of Lebanon—they fashioned ships that could carry between one and two hundred tons of goods.

Long-distance "Tarshish" ships were armed and driven by two banks of oarsmen. A smaller model hugged the coast and a third was used for ferrying. Traders rowed by daylight only, thus necessitating closely spaced ports. And whoever held ports controlled trade along the coasts.

The Phoenicians were intrepid sailors, broadening the limits of the known world by venturing past the Pillars of Hercules at Gibraltar and by circumnavigating Africa in three years around 600 B.C. They were also resolute warriors, but fell to the Assyrians, who punished them by razing the Phoenician capital at Sidon and taking much of their profits in taxes. Under the rule of the Persians, however, the Phoenician fleets received better treatment.

*This painted terra-cotta vase (above) from the tenth century B.C. was made by Phoenician potters who were familiar with both Egyptian and Mesopotamian ware. Below, a bas-relief made in the thirteenth century B.C. depicting an Egyptian-style funeral feast on the sarcophagus of King Ahiram of Byblos. It carries an inscription in alphabetic writing, which the Phoenicians were the first to employ. Their exposure to difficult Egyptian hieroglyphs and Mesopotamian cuneiform may have led them to invent their "shorthand."*

The cedar of Lebanon (above) is an evergreen with a wide trunk, providing a sweet-smelling wood. The Sumerian hero Gilgamesh and his hairy alter ego Enkidu traveled far up the Euphrates to seek out this tree. Later Mesopotamian kings would have the cedars felled and floated down river. The Phoenicians were master shipbuilders who fashioned from their cedars such ships as this commercial vessel (left) carved on a second century B.C. sarcophagus from Sidon, their capital.

Below, an earlier Phoenician ship is shown. It belonged to Sennacherib's fleet and was carved in relief at Nineveh during the ninth century B.C. The rowers are seen at work; above them, but not shown, hang the shields of the soldiers who often stood on deck during the sail. The Phoenicians sometimes sacrificed to their gods in rectangular altars such as this, below center. Food, drink, birds, animals, and even infants fed the fires.

duced some refined gold and silver coins—an improvement of the unrefined "Ishtar heads" that the Assyrians had made—Darius revolutionized business by putting out standard gold *darics* (daric means gold). These coins were ninety-eight percent gold and were stamped with a kneeling archer—an image of Darius himself. Since only the king could make darics, they were absolutely uniform and took the mistrust out of purchasing.

Although the common man was usually paid in meat, wine, grain, or other goods, state taxes were payable in coins or metal objects. These were melted down each year at Persepolis or Susa and stored as ingots. When the great treasure house at Persepolis was finally opened by the Greeks in 330 B.C., there were 270 tons of gold coins and 1,200 tons of silver ingots. The removal of so much money from circulation had damaged the economy. Ingenious as they were, Darius's reforms brought inflation, and the value of the talent halved in the short two-hundred-year history of the empire. Hardly unusual in our era, such an occurrence in the context of an ordinarily stable barter economy is remarkable.

In the sciences, Pasargadae and Ecbatana were as arid as their plateau, but the Achaemenid Empire brought together the three great traditions of Mesopotamia, Egypt, and Greece. Centuries of observing the sky and recording its movement had led to the adoption of a twelve-month year in Mesopotamia, modified by an extra month whenever the seasons seemed out of synchronization. A hexagesimal number system, the first known to employ place value, had produced the 360-degree circle and the 60-minute hour. The Babylonians could figure squares, roots, areas, and volumes. In about 375 B.C., a Babylonian named Kidinnu, or Cidenas, figured the length of the year with outstanding accuracy. The Egyptians had a decimal system and a mathematics that surpassed that of the Babylonians in some respects. They studied the human body and took pulses, considering the heart a pump. They knew something of blood circulation and the function of the brain. Democritus of Thrace proposed that the

*Right, a detail from a large gold plate of the sixth century B.C. showing two rams with interlocked horns. Among the first animals to be domesticated, the ram was also early deified. Here the attempt seems not so much to deify as to make the rams kingly: they are given a royal air and curly, square-cut beards similar to those worn by the Persian monarchs.*

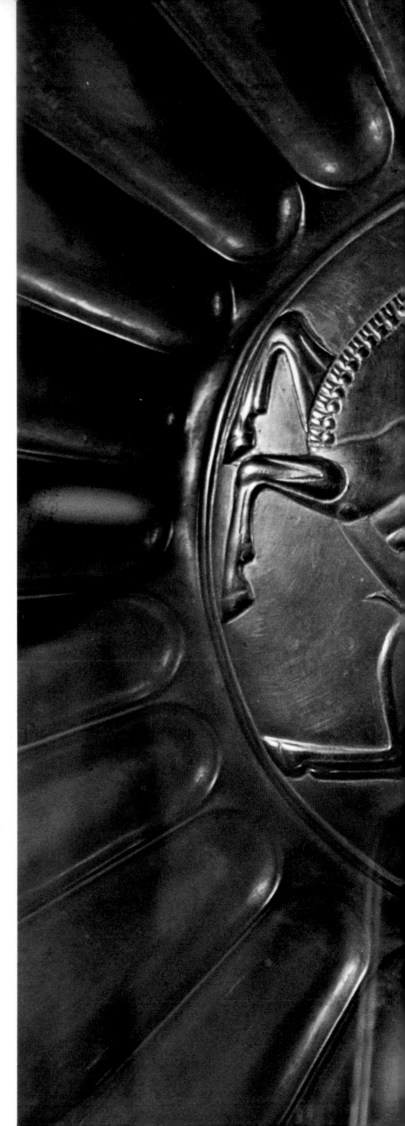

unchanging elements in the world were small bits of matter called atoms. Near the Ionian coast on the island of Cos was a great medical school, its library full of diagnostic books, each with careful observations and intelligent theories, which would one day be inaccurately ascribed to a single doctor, Hippocrates.

It was thus under the Persian Empire that a world culture first arose, a child of countless local traditions. There were dozens of satraps or minor kings, but only one great king of kings; there were local gods, but gaining strength all the time was the idea of one god; there were many tablets of laws, but one imperial legal system; many languages, but the single official Aramaic; and various coins, but one official currency.

Xerxes was murdered in his bed by his chief bodyguard in 465 B.C., and after him came five weak, if violent, kings who were ineffectual against a relentless cycle of loss and corruption. Considerable amounts of gold went west to Greece as bribes to keep its various cities from uniting and rebelling. Tariffs and taxes and duties of all kinds increased, and inflation soared. Revolt in the satrapies continued, and the kings grew simultaneously more repressive and less successful.

*Left, a fluted silver amphora dating from the fifth or fourth century B.C. On its handles are horse heads. Right, two bronze lions used as the knobs at the ends of chair arms. Persian artists would take naturalistic figures from Assyrian models and maintain a stylized form throughout all their pieces: the facial muscles of all the lions on this page provide a good example of this.*

*A bronze mirror back (left) made in the fifth or fourth century B.C. is decorated with snarling lions. The bronze weight (below) in the shape of a lion comes from Susa. Weights usually bore the name of the king during whose reign they were cast.*

Persians could now avoid military service by cash payment, and the army, as a result, became almost totally mercenary.

In 135 years of decline, the Persian kings almost continually shifted alliances in an attempt to sidestep an invasion by Greece. Artaxerxes I (465–432) fought off an Egyptian-Athenian coalition and courted Athens himself. Darius II (432–404) kept mostly to court, lost Egypt, and joined in league with Sparta when the Ionian cities revolted again. Artaxerxes II (404–359) lost quite a few satrapies and fought with Sparta. Artaxerxes III (359–338) managed to win back Egypt, but by the time of his successor there was little empire left.

When the next king, Darius III, first sat upon the throne of Persia in 336 B.C., he was already middle aged. His court was as glamorous as any Achaemenid's, but for the common people, life was far from luxurious. Persia's economic system was basically feudal, with landowners growing richer and peasants poorer. The peasants dreaded progress, as it meant enforced labor on roads and buildings. In some ways, it was better to be a slave than a freeman. Impover-

*Ten and a half inches high and made of silver and gold, this winged ibex (left) once served as the handle of an Achaemenid drinking vessel. The figure's position and the shape of its wings show Greek influence. The wine-shunning Persians eventually became great drinkers and custom dictated important decisions be pondered twice: first sober, then drunk. The coins (below) are famous gold darics with a figure of a kneeling archer, shown about three times actual size.*

*The four tombs at Naqsh-i-Rustam, eight miles northeast of Persepolis (top and preceding pages), contain Darius I, and probably Xerxes I, Artaxerxes I, and Darius II. Immediately above, the sarcophagus of Darius, carved into the rock in situ. Darius may well rest in peace, as his inscription reads "I am not hot-tempered. What things develop in my anger, I hold firmly under control by my thinking power."*

*Right, one of the blind windows framed in black limestone from the side of the Fire Temple (far right).*

ished and overtaxed Persians of the fourth century B.C. longed for a savior just as Babylonians had once longed for Cyrus.

Far to the northwest across the Mediterranean, a twenty-one-year-old king was collecting an army of thirty-five thousand men. Handsome and charismatic, he was the son of a man who had somewhat brutally mastered and confederated the quarreling city-states of mainland Greece. As Cyrus of Persis had taken Babylon, Alexander and his father had come from the rustic province of Macedon in 338 B.C. to seize Athens. When Philip was murdered, Alexander proclaimed himself king of the Greeks. The federation of Greek cities began to fall apart. Violently and somewhat grotesquely, Alexander reunited it—curbing rebellion in Thebes by destroying the city to the accompaniment of flutes. That music would be heard again in Persia, Alexander's next conquest.

As Xerxes had done before him, Alexander poured wine and dropped a golden goblet into the sea at the Hellespont, and in the spring of 334 B.C., the Greeks disembarked in Asia Minor. The clean-shaven Macedonian soldiers wore reinforced armor and carried fourteen-foot spears and short swords at their belts. Their shields were of thick looped metal and their breastplates of overlapping metal scales. The foot soldiers marched in the tight formation of overlapping shields and long spears developed by Philip called the phalanx. They used iron-tipped, wheeled battering rams, enormous siege towers, and catapults powered by twisted ropes of hair, which were capable of hurling burning spears or fifty-pound stones.

In Persia proper, the king of kings did not comprehend Alexander's strength, nor did his military advisers closer to the invaders in Lydia, Ionia, and Phrygia. The Persians had not seen Alexander in battle. When Darius III finally arrived with his armies, which included many Greek mercenaries, to meet Alexander at the Granicus River, the Persians found that there was not enough room to maneuver their cavalry. Furthermore, they were blinded by the

*Left, the white limestone Fire Temple at Naqsh-i-Rustam, built in front of the tomb of Darius I. In it burned the eternal fire, tended by priests, the only ones allowed inside. Ceremonies were held in the open air and fire brought from the tower to exterior altars. On one side of the temple, a stairway led to the raised entrance, while the other three sides contained blind windows. In later times, the temple may have held a statue of the goddess Anahita, lady of the waters, with her crown of 108-rayed stars.*

# On the road . . .
# to Susa

There were roads across the Iranian plateau, the Mesopotamian plain, and the Anatolian peninsula long before there was a Persian Empire. Cyrus and Darius employed numerous engineers to improve them, laying paving over unstable marsh land, cutting out curves, and smoothing surfaces. The empire's great Royal Road ran from central Susa to provincial Sardes, a stretch of almost 1,600 miles; those who traveled this route had to cross four rivers and climb numerous mountains.

Distances were measured in *parasangs,* or the three-plus miles a person can walk in an hour. Eighteen miles was considered a day's walk and inns were spaced a day apart—in the mountains they were closer. Soldiers and inspectors were stationed on the busy road, too, and fresh horses waited beside riders ready to relay fast messages. The Persians refined a "Pony Express" system begun by the kings of Akkad and Assyria. Persian couriers were able to make the three-month walking trip from Sardes to Susa in only seven days.

*The Royal Road of the Persians wound its way through hill country (above right) at Katakekauneme near Ankara in the middle of the Anatolian peninsula. Eastward the road crossed the Halys River and continued on to Susa, now in ruins (below). At Susa, the road was met by another from Babylon. A branch of the Royal Road ran off from Ankara southeast to what would soon be the city of Alexandretta, over landscape like that shown below right.*

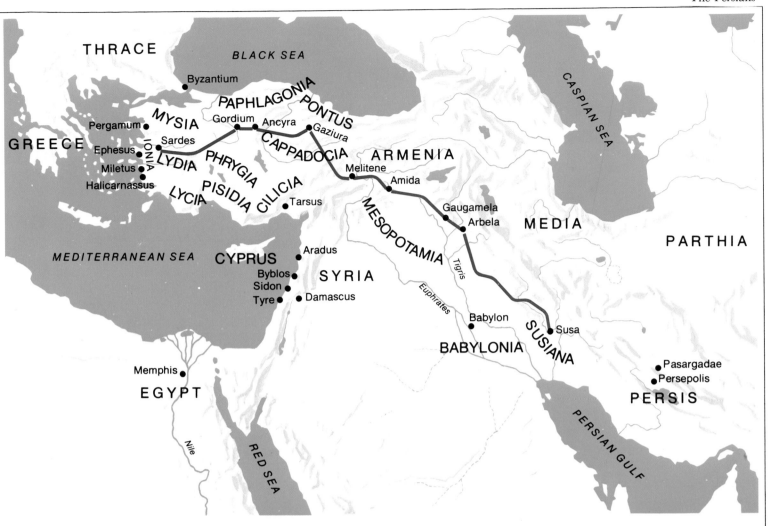

One reason King Midas was so rich was that his city of Gordium (below left) lay on an ancient road by the banks of the only Anatolian river navigable by light craft. The Royal Road took the same path. The roadway began (or ended) at the base of the acropolis, the site of the shrine of Cybele in Sardes (below right). Tradition has it that Greeks settled Sardes and mixed with local peoples during Homeric times.

*Greek and Persian styles appear together in this marble stele from about 400 B.C. (above) found in Phrygia. In the hunting scene at the top, the garments are Persian, as are the trappings worn by the horse. Funerary steles were themselves unknown in Persia, and the sumptuous funeral banquet at the bottom takes place in a Greek setting. Though they appear on the same stele, the two styles remain distinct.*

northward along the Euphrates. In Syria, he headed into the hills by the Mediterranean and put himself west of Alexander to block the young king's return to Europe.

But Alexander had not been thinking of flight—he had gone down to the plains to hunt Darius. When Alexander came back up into the hills in the late autumn, he found Darius only a mile and a half from the Mediterranean, on the fields of Issus. Darius was trapped once again in an area too small for maneuvering his cavalry. Though the Greek phalanxes were at first dwarfed by the enormous number of Persian troops, Alexander led a lusty charge straight in the face of the generals. Darius, watching from his golden chariot, decided that, for the good of Persia, he should call for flight. He then ordered the royal charioteer to leave the field, abandoning his wife, mother, and two daughters. When Alexander later prowled through their tent, examining the bathtubs and basins, the perfumes and ointments, he is said to have remarked: "This, it seems, is royalty."

Darius sent Alexander a polite letter offering to ransom his family, to which Alexander is said to have replied: "Whatever you ask for, you will receive; and nothing shall be denied you. But for the future, whenever you send to me, send to me as the king of Asia . . . and if you dispute my right to the kingdom, stay and fight another battle for it; but do not run away."

Darius gave up the correspondence. In a few months, he was receiving reports that Alexander had gone against the double-fortressed city of Tyre in Phoenicia. The Macedonians easily took the fort on the Phoenician coast, but the one built on an island off the coast was thought to be unassailable. Darius assumed that Alexander's attempt to take what no

afternoon sun. In hand-to-hand combat, Alexander and his men killed twelve thousand Persians and captured another twenty thousand, as well as two thousand Greek mercenaries. Alexander promptly sold the mercenaries into slavery and proclaimed himself liberator of the Greek cities of Asia.

Miletus would not open its gates, so Alexander led another successful attack, and Darius soon heard that he had finally lost the key city of Ionia. He was advised that, this time, the young Greek king had wisely increased his force by hiring the Greek mercenaries who had turned themselves over to him. At his winter palace in Susa, Darius began to assemble as large an army as he could. In the summer of 333, his cumbersome collection of soldiers, elephants, scythed chariots, shopkeepers, and children progressed slowly

*Not far from where Alexander the Great crossed from Europe into Asia, the peaceful, now abandoned, acropolis of Assos (above right) was once the site of a Doric temple to Athena built in 540 B.C. The sixth century B.C. coin (near right) showing Tyche crowned is from Smyrna in Ionia. In 600 B.C., Smyrna was conquered by the Lydians, from whom the Persians would later learn the art of coining money. Far right, two small coins from Miletus and two larger ones from Ephesus and Tarsus. The fourth century B.C. Ephesus coin shows the forepart of a stag, emblem of Artemis. The Tarsus coin shows a lion on the back of a falling stag, a motif which goes as far back as 1500 B.C. The world's first known coins depicted the head of the sun god Shamash and were made in Mesopotamia, ca. 2000 B.C.*

man had taken before would give the Persians sufficient time to assemble enough soldiers to replace the many thousands lost at Issus. As summer turned to autumn, however, Darius heard that Alexander was using the rubble of mainland Tyre to build a mole half a mile into the sea toward the island. Then the king received word that eighty of his own Phoenician ships had gone over to Alexander. By winter, Alexander had indeed broken the island stronghold and sold its thirty thousand women and children as slaves. No men of Tyre survived.

At Gaza, there were no survivors whatsoever. Darius received word that his Persian authorities in Egypt had opened the satrapy's treasures to the triumphant Greeks. On the Nile, Alexander proclaimed that the ram-headed god Zeus-Amon had given him victory. Cheered on by the Egyptians, Alexander sprinkled flour into the black earth of the Nile delta to mark the site of one of the nineteen cities he would build for himself in his conquered territories: Today it is known as Alexandria. In Cyrene, administrators submitted, and the western edge of the Persian Empire was gone.

In the spring of 331 B.C., the last of the Achaemenids took two thousand four-horse chariots and a force of nearly two hundred thousand warriors up the embankment of the Tigris to Gaugamela in Assyria. Darius cleared a wide area on the plain, intending to avoid being caught on a small field. The battle began, and the Greeks lured the chariots to rougher ground, where they careened helplessly against each other. Alexander, wearing a jeweled collar and a white plumed iron helmet, rode with his men. His tight-fitting breastplate of quilted linen was Persian—captured at Issus.

Despite the tradition that the Persian king should only watch battles from the royal chariot, Darius flung a spear at his approaching enemy, but he missed. As Alexander rushed onward, Darius jumped from his chariot onto a fast horse and was gone. The Persian forces scattered. Alexander followed, but Darius was on the road to Ecbatana with his Greek mercenaries and the Persian and Bactrian cavalry, which were about all he had left in the world. Alexander turned back to the plain and went south.

He was greeted in Babylon with flowers and incense. Like Cyrus in so many ways, Alexander had forbidden his soldiers to plunder the city. Indeed, he honored the Babylonian god Bel-Marduk and elected a Persian viceroy to govern Babylonia. Then Susa opened its arms to Alexander. Next, he turned southeast, crossing the Zagros Mountains in winter. His men faced blizzards and cold, but they suffered most

from their hunger for plunder. Darius's garrison commander turned Persepolis over to Alexander without a fight, and the Macedonians grabbed so much loot that one soldier had silver nails made for his boots. According to one version of the story, when a drunken Greek courtesan asked Alexander to burn Persepolis, he agreed. To the tune of drums and flutes, he and his men set fire to the great tapestries and the brilliant hangings in the palace. The flames that roared up the cedar pillars were so hot that the iron spearheads in the palace storeroom actually fused together.

When the Greeks reached Ecbatana in the spring of 330 B.C., Darius was fleeing into the Elburz Mountains south of the Caspian with his Bactrian cavalry. Here the victory of Bactria had turned against him and wounded him. Darius was put into an empty cart—no golden bowls, no servants to fetch the water that his thirst demanded, no friends. Finally, as he lay dying, Darius saw the faces of Alexander's advance guard. The soldiers gave him water and begged him to stay alive until Alexander, who greatly respected Darius and the Persian royal line, could reach him. But by the time Alexander arrived, there was nothing to do but cover the body with the royal purple cloak and order that the great king be carried back to the ruins of Persepolis for burial.

On his way home, the new king of kings, Alexander the Great, staged a mass marriage of Persian noblewomen and Macedonian army officers, in hopes of breeding Persian sophistication with Greek vitality and forming a true empire. But with his death, his realm would be tested, and the vulnerable coalition of tribute states would prove as difficult to rule as it had under the Persians. When Alexander burned Persepolis, the ceremonial capital, he in effect destroyed the soul of the empire. For even in the best of times, when long processions of tribute-bearers paid homage to the great Persian kings, the power of the empire must have seemed somewhat illusory.

*King of the world, Alexander the Great of Macedon is portrayed in the bust at right. Before he died in Babylon at thirty-three, Alexander united Asia and Europe as no Achaemenid had been able to do. The Macedonian longed to push eastward through Asia to the edge of the world—partly so he could inform his tutor Aristotle of what he had found there. But his exhausted soldiers refused to follow him after crossing the Indus River: unlike the Achaemenids, the Macedonian kings were held in check by a new force—freemen.*

# Imperial Greece

The area now known as Greece saw the comings and goings of many people before it was inhabited by the Greeks we read about so often today. Tribes wandered onto the Greek mainland as early as 7000 B.C. (during the Paleolithic period), but the area's first continuous settlements were not founded until the Neolithic period, ca. 6500 B.C. The identity of these early settlers of Greece remains a mystery, but they were not direct ancestors of those we usually call the Greeks.

Greece witnessed its second wave of migrations by at least 1900 B.C. The newcomers, who most probably swept in from the north, either overpowered or simply mingled with the earlier settlers. Whether the new

*The Temple of Poseidon (preceding page) rises on the pinnacle of Cape Sounion, the outermost point of Attica in the Aegean Sea. The Athenians built the temple around 440 B.C. when their empire was at its peak, and Sounion served them as a naval base. A stretch of seacoast (top) and a gorge in Arcadia (above), a mountainous region of the Peloponnesus, exemplify the fragmentary nature of the terrain that so influenced the history of the Greek people.*

peoples came in violence or peace, their religious beliefs appear to have blended compatibly with those of the first inhabitants: The migrants gave priority to a sky god, while the settled people assigned dominance to a nature goddess. The new religion accepted both.

With these newcomers came the early trappings of what would become the language of classical Greece. Springing from the Indo-European family of languages, which includes the Germanic, Italic, Slavic, Celtic, Persian, and Hittite languages, this early Greek would later develop into the language that best defined the Greeks as a separate and distinct people.

The new language contributed to the development of a culture that assimilated customs and beliefs of both the newcomers and the indigenous people. By about 1600 B.C., the new inhabitants had begun to build a series of palace-fortresses ruled by warrior-chieftains at Argos, Pylos, Thebes, Sparta, and Athens. The most impressive, and ultimately the most consequential of the palaces, was built at Mycenae. This Mycenaean citadel would eventually lend its name to the emergent culture, a culture remembered for its great chamber tombs, lavish use of gold, and preoccupation with conquest.

For all their achievements, the Mycenaeans remained a rather basic culture compared to such advanced contemporaries as the Babylonians and the Egyptians. Even on the island of Crete, the non-Greek people had long since fashioned a sophisticated civilization, known as the Minoan. The Minoans took their name from the title assigned to each of their kings upon assuming the throne—minos. So far-reaching were the Minoans' contacts in the Mediterranean that centuries later the historian Thucydides wrote (Book I, Chap. 1): "Minos, according to tradition, was the first person to organize a navy. He controlled the greater part of the Aegean Sea and ruled over Cyclades, in most of which he founded the first colonies and put in his sons as governors."

Although the Minoans did not exercise absolute military, political, or administrative control over non-Minoan peoples, they were indisputably a commercial and cultural presence in the eastern Mediterranean. It is difficult to determine what degree of political control they exercised, but the famous legend of the Athenian king Theseus facing the Minotaur on Crete certainly suggests that the Minoans were sufficiently organized to be able to exert some domination over mainland Greece.

The tables eventually turned on the Minoans. By ca. 1450 B.C., the Mycenaeans appear to have taken over at least the main palace-centers on Crete. This is often attested to by the appearance of Linear B script on Crete at this time. The Mycenaeans used Linear B,

an early form of the language that would become Greek, to record their language, and it in turn reflected a Greek culture: One tablet, for example, described offerings to deities named Zeus, Hera, and Hermes.

In addition to taking over Crete, the Mycenaeans replaced the Minoans as the proprietors of commerce and culture in the eastern Mediterranean. Although it is difficult to say just how well developed their imperial ambitions were, it seems that the Mycenaeans had attained sufficient size to launch a punitive expedition against Troy (as recounted in the *Iliad* and the *Odyssey*) sometime between 1270 and 1190 B.C.

Whatever the attack on Troy represented, the Mycenaean culture must have already been on the decline by this time, for in the ensuing decades, several Mycenaean citadels were destroyed. At Pylos, Linear B tablets recorded last-minute efforts to organize a defense: "The watchers are guarding the coastal regions." But the vigil was not enough to save Pylos. By 1100 B.C., Mycenae itself was destroyed.

*Above, the view from Delphi to the valley of the Pleistos River, with a bay in the Gulf of Corinth seen in the distance. The pre-Hellenistic sanctuary at Delphi developed through the Mycenaean period to become a sanctuary of Apollo, which by 550 B.C. served as a religious and spiritual center for all the Greeks.*

The successors, and perhaps the destroyers, of the Mycenaeans were the Dorians, another group of Greek-speaking people. Like earlier migrants they appear to have come down via northern Greece to settle in central and southern Greece. Some Dorians made their way across to Crete and took over what was left of the Minoan-Mycenaean realm.

The Dorians did not attempt to conquer all of Greece but left small pockets of Mycenaeans untouched, the most significant of which was in Attica, where Athens became a city of refuge. Various My-

# Athenian supremacy and the Greek world

## Leaders

Cecrops—first king of Athens / Pandion—son of Cecrops / Erechtheus and Aegeus—sons of Pandion / Theseus—son of Aegeus / Draco—first lawgiver / Solon—archon, lawgiver, and reformer / Pisistratus—tyrant, war hero, leader of poor people / Hippias and Hipparchus—tyrants / Cleisthenes—lawgiver and reformer / Miltiades—general, victor of the battle of Marathon / Themistocles—archon, soldier, and statesman; promoter of Athens' naval power / Aristides—archon, statesman, and general during the Persian wars / Cimon—general, statesman, and political leader / Pericles—general; dominated Athenian politics during the middle part of the fifth century B.C. / Cleon—general; political leader during the Peloponnesian War / Nicias—general; upheld a policy of prudence during the war with Sparta / Alcibiades—statesman, general, and political leader / Demosthenes—orator and political leader

## Political Events

Unification of the twelve Attica townships under Athenian monarchal leadership in the thirteenth century B.C.; usually attributed to Theseus. Suppression of the monarchy (tenth century B.C.) and institution of an oligarchic government led by archons. Political life dominated by the landowning *eupatrids* (nobles) and by the Alcmaeonids (patrician family, eighth-seventh centuries B.C.) Promulgation of strict written laws by Draco (621 B.C.). Legislative and political reform by Solon (594 B.C.). Pisistratus institutes several populist reforms (560–527 B.C.). Democratic reforms by Cleisthenes (508 B.C.). Athens builds a powerful fleet under Themistocles (493–480 B.C.). The victory over Persia off Salamis (480 B.C.) increases Athenian prestige, and the Delian League is formed to contain Persian expansion (478–477 B.C.). Under Pericles, Athens transforms the Delian League into an effective Athenian commercial empire (454 B.C.). Plague in Athens in 430 B.C. Death of Pericles in 429 B.C. Athens, defeated in the Peloponnesian War (404 B.C.), is forced to submit to the oligarchy of the Thirty Tyrants imposed by Sparta; they are expelled in 403 B.C. by Thrasybulus. Socrates brought to trial and condemned to death in 399 B.C. Led by Demosthenes, Athens opposes the hegemonic ambitions of Philip II of Macedon in 350 B.C. After the battle of Chaeronea in 338 B.C., Athens becomes part of the Macedonian League of Corinth.

## Military Events

Battle of Marathon (490 B.C.); Athenians defeat the Persians. Destruction of Athens by the Persians in 480 B.C. Naval victory at Salamis over the Persians in 480 B.C. Greek victories at Plataea and Mycale over the Persians in 479 B.C. The Athenians, led by Cimon, defeat the Persians at Eurymedon in 466 B.C. Peace of Callias between Athens and Persia in 449 B.C. Differences between Athens and Sparta provoke the Peloponnesian War (431–404 B.C.), which involves all of Greece. The Athenians are defeated by the Spartans in the battle of Aegospotami in 405 B.C. In 404 B.C., Athens surrenders to Sparta. Thebes crushes Sparta in the battle of Leuctra in 371 B.C.. Macedonians defeat a force of Athenians and Thebans at the battle of Chaeronea (338 B.C.).

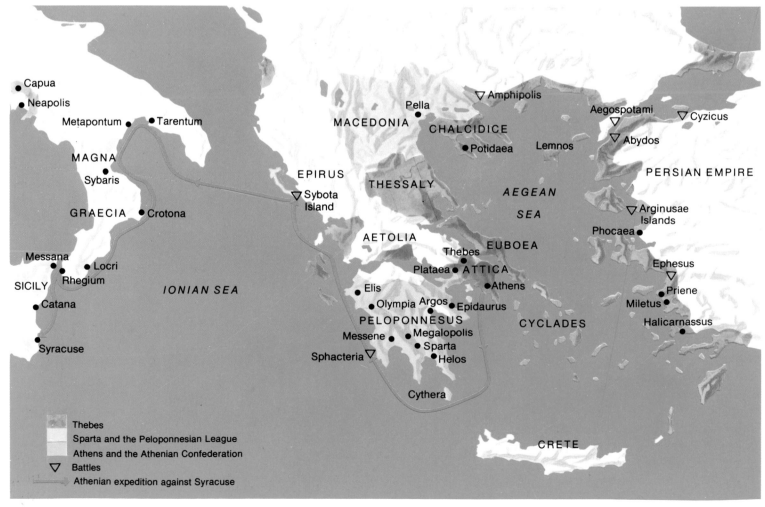

Legend:
- Thebes
- Sparta and the Peloponnesian League
- Athens and the Athenian Confederation
- ▽ Battles
- Athenian expedition against Syracuse

# The Greek world during Spartan ascendency

## Leaders

Lycurgus / Chilon / Leonidas / Euribiades / Pausanias / Leotychides / Lysander / Agesilaus II / Agis III

## Political Events

Sparta is founded by Dorians, ca. tenth century B.C. Constitution is drawn up during the eighth or seventh century B.C. Sparta forms military alliances with city-states of the Peloponnesus in the sixth century B.C. Persia and Sparta sign Treaty of Antalcidas in 387 B.C.

## Military Events

Sparta gains total control in Messenian Wars (ca. 730 B.C.). Peloponnesian War (431–404 B.C.) Spartan victory at Coronea over Athens and Thebes (394 B.C.). In the battle of Leuctra (371 B.C.), Sparta surrenders to Thebes. Spartans contain Theban supremacy at Mantinea in 362 B.C.

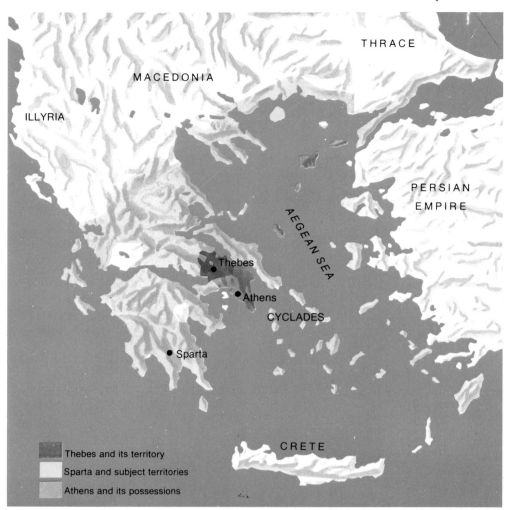

Thebes and its territory
Sparta and subject territories
Athens and its possessions

# The Theban domain in the Greek world

## Leaders

Cadmus / Laius / Oedipus / Eteocles / Polynices / Antigone / Leontiadas / Pelopidas / Epaminondas

## Political Events

In the sixth century B.C., Thebes becomes the leading city in Boeotia. After the Greek victory over the Persians, Thebes submits to severe conditions but is saved by Sparta from complete destruction. In 378 B.C., the Spartans are expelled.

## Military Events

Theban attack on Athenians at Plataea in 431 B.C. causes Peloponnesian War. After the war, Thebes expels Sparta, and open war breaks out in 371 B.C. At the battle of Leuctra, the Thebans defeat the Spartans. Battle of Mantinea in 362 B.C. proves indecisive. Alexander the Great destroys Thebes in 336 B.C.

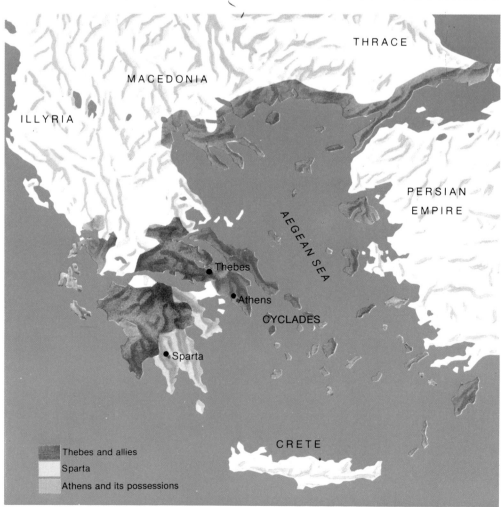

Thebes and allies
Sparta
Athens and its possessions

The main approach (below) to the acropolis at Mycenae leads through the Lion Gate (left) to the citadel of one of the most important centers of preclassical Greece (from about 1600 to 1100 B.C.).

*"Tiryns of the great walls" is how Homer spoke of this great citadel (left), a contemporary of nearby Mycenae. Its walls—originally up to sixty-five feet high, with individual blocks some three feet thick and six feet long—prompted later Greeks to attribute this and similar structures to the Cyclopes, mythical one-eyed giants. Another legend claimed that Tiryns was the home of Heracles, the hero whose feats projected a similar image of supernatural strength.*

*Right, the remains from the archaic and classical periods of the Sanctuary of Hera, tutelary goddess of the plain dominated by the citadels at Argos and Mycenae. It was at this sanctuary that Agamemnon is said to have been chosen leader of the expedition to Troy, and the sanctuary continued to play an important role long after the end of the Mycenaean civilization.*

cenaeans met the Dorian threat by staking out new settlements across the Aegean. Many settled on the coast of Asia Minor and its off-shore islands, where they took over the land—often by force—from the indigenous people. In the next centuries, Attica Mycenaeans developed the prosperous and progressive Ionian culture on Asia Minor that arose, at least, in some respects, ahead of the civilization of the mainland Greeks.

According to legend, the Dorians gained control of mainland Greece by 1104 B.C. From this point on, the Greeks commonly referred to themselves as Hellenes. They were a primitive tribal people and could be considered backward even in an era when much of the known world was in a cultural eclipse. At the hands of the Dorians, Greece fell into a "dark age" for the next three centuries, during which there were only scanty indications of cultural development.

One exception to the darkness of the era was the art of pottery. The ancients always needed pottery and the tradition of painted ceramics continued, especially at Athens. For the most part during this period, however, the Dorians had few contacts with the world outside Greece. Life centered around basic subsistence at the village level. Land was the sole measure of wealth and power, and the landed families who

displaced the warrior-chieftains aspired to little more than self-sufficient domains, petty in size and outlook. This naturally increased fragmentation among all Greeks.

If these centuries were a time of parochialism in one respect, they were also a time of consolidation. A common Greek "consciousness" was evolving, nurtured by one language and one religion. As Herodotus put it, these widely dispersed Greeks had a sense of "being of the same stock and the same speech," and of having "common shrines of the gods and rivals." At the same time, the impoverished rural populations were becoming restless under the stagnant social and political system that favored the land-rich. Many of the disadvantaged moved to the expanding cities, most near the coast, where they found employment in urban and commercial trades. Commerce brought contacts with non-Greek peoples and, with it, a broader sense of the world and its possibilities.

By the mid-eighth century B.C., the Greeks had begun to emerge as a political and cultural power. They were sufficiently organized—and had sufficient need—to embark upon a series of migrations into the Mediterranean and to the Black Sea. The impulse was partly necessity—a response to scarcity of land on

# Homer and the *Iliad*

The *Iliad* is the story of the Greek hero Achilles and the consequences of his wrath. The epic relates an episode in the history of the Trojan War, a conflict instigated when Helen, wife of the Greek king Menelaus, is abducted by the Trojan Paris. Achilles quarrels with Agamemnon, brother of Menelaus, and refuses to fight, nearly causing the Greeks to lose the war. Eventually, Achilles relents and leads them to victory, killing Hector and bringing the downfall of the Trojan kingdom.

Although most scholars today agree the *Iliad* and the *Odyssey* were written by the same man—Homer—some contend both works could only have been the result of multiple authorship. In fact, the two views may be reconciled. The epic of the Trojan War was sung countless times by countless singers before it reached Homer. A tradition of oral poets extending back into pre-literate Bronze Age Greece handed the story down from generation to generation. Homer, however, was probably the first to set the *Iliad* down in writing, thus getting credit for authorship.

*Right, the protagonist of the* Iliad, *Achilles, depicted on an amphora of the fifth century B.C. It was his wrath over being deprived of a captured maiden that culminated in his killing Hector. Possibly based on a real Mycenaean warrior, the legend of Achilles spread throughout the Greek world along with the popularity of the* Iliad.

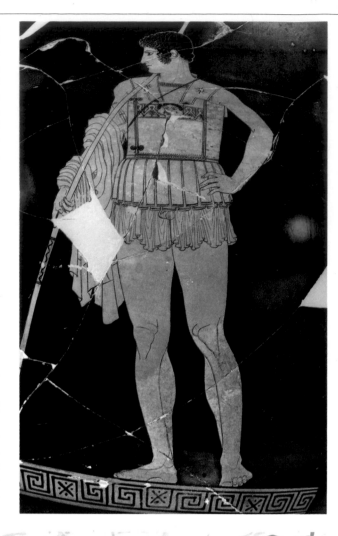

*One of the most celebrated sections of the* Iliad *is "the catalogue of ships" in Book II, which lists the various contingents that banded together for the expedition to Troy. The map (below) draws on this and other references to Homer to show the Greek world of about 1300 B.C. Modern archaeology has generally confirmed the existence of much of this Homeric world.*

*Nothing was known of Homer's life, let alone his appearance, but the bust (above) follows the tradition that he was blind. The ideal of the blind bard reflects the belief that such men developed their powers of memory and speech along with the power of an inner sight—all Homer's strengths.*

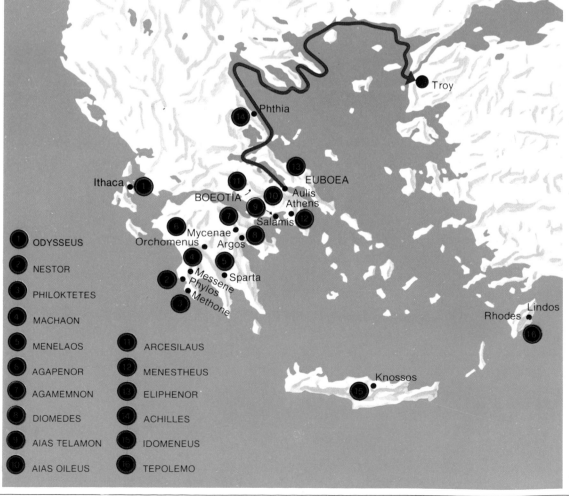

1. ODYSSEUS
2. NESTOR
3. PHILOKTETES
4. MACHAON
5. MENELAOS
6. AGAPENOR
7. AGAMEMNON
8. DIOMEDES
9. AIAS TELAMON
10. AIAS OILEUS
11. ARCESILAUS
12. MENESTHEUS
13. ELIPHENOR
14. ACHILLES
15. IDOMENEUS
16. TEPOLEMO

Right, a painting on a red-figured drinking cup, or kylix, of Helen, wife of Menelaus of Sparta. She is serving Priam, king of Troy and father of Paris, whose abduction of Helen sparked the Greek's expedition against Troy. Helen became for the Greeks the epitome of a wronged woman.

It was customary in ancient times to strip a dead warrior, and this fifth century B.C. vase painting (below) shows Greeks and Trojans fighting over the armor of the dead Achilles outside walls similar to those (below right) of Troy VI, the sixth major citadel on this site.

Vase paintings show the sorceress Circe offering Odysseus a drugged potion (below) that turns men into swine, the fate of his companions (below center). Odysseus foiled Circe's designs with the aid of an herb, an example of his proverbial cunning.

# The *Odyssey*

Odysseus' ten-year struggle to return home to his wife and son in Greece after the sack of Troy dominates the *Odyssey,* Homer's second epic. A central part of the *Odyssey* also describes how Odysseus' son, Telemachus, responds to the challenge of his father's absence and grows to manhood.

The *Odyssey,* which came out of the same oral tradition that produced the *Iliad,* contains many motifs and episodes discovered in the epics of other preliterate cultures. For example, Odysseus' final return to Ithaca—during which he disguises himself as a shepherd to surprise his wife who believes him dead—has an almost identical counterpart in Yugoslavian oral tradition, which died out only recently.

*One of the best-known episodes of the* Odyssey *was the blinding of the one-eyed Cyclops, Polyphemus, by Odysseus and his men in order to escape from the giant's cave. Evidence of the widespread popularity of this and other episodes from the Homeric epics is the painting (above) on a black-figured* hydria, *or water jug, ca. 520 B.C., found in Caere, an Etruscan city in Italy.*

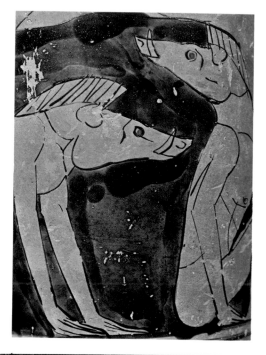

*The red-figured vase painting of ca. 440 B.C. shows (below left) Penelope, wife of Odysseus, and their son, Telemachus. On the other side of the vase (below right) is Odysseus, who has returned to Ithaca disguised as a beggar. He is recognized by his old nurse, Eurycleia, when she sees a childhood wound while washing his feet.*

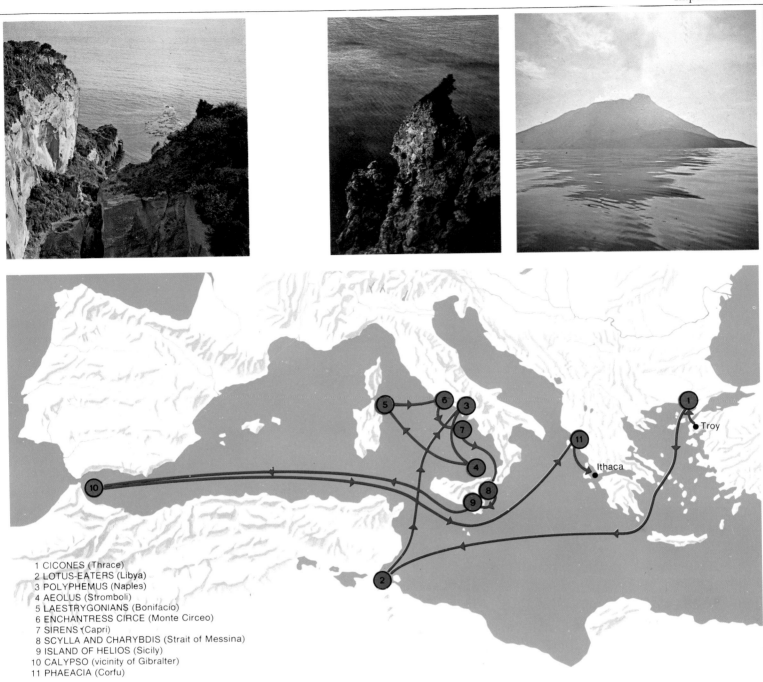

1 CICONES (Thrace)
2 LOTUS-EATERS (Libya)
3 POLYPHEMUS (Naples)
4 AEOLUS (Stromboli)
5 LAESTRYGONIANS (Bonifacio)
6 ENCHANTRESS CIRCE (Monte Circeo)
7 SIRENS (Capri)
8 SCYLLA AND CHARYBDIS (Strait of Messina)
9 ISLAND OF HELIOS (Sicily)
10 CALYPSO (vicinity of Gibralter)
11 PHAEACIA (Corfu)

From ancient times, attempts have been made to reconstruct Odysseus' itinerary, and the map (above) is only one of many such attempts. Among the places suggested as figuring in Homer's epic are (top, left to right): the grotto of Posillipo, near Naples, as the cave of Polyphemus; the Sicilian side of the Strait of Messina, as the petrified monster Scylla that faced the whirlpool Charybdis; the volcanic island Stromboli, as the home of Aeolus, king of the winds; and (below left) Corfu, as Scheria, home of Nausicaa. Only Ithaca (below right) has been universally identified as the home of Odysseus.

the mainland, a changing social structure, and the impoverishment of growing numbers of small farmers—and partly exploratory. Colonizing expeditions from individual cities traveled west to Sicily, southern Italy, Massilia (now Marseille) on the coast of France, the Balearic Islands, and the Mediterranean coast of Spain. To the south, the colonists founded Cyrene (modern Libya), and even in Egypt, at Naucratis on the Nile delta, they were permitted to set up a special trading outpost. The eastern coast of the Mediterranean was already settled, but the Greeks moved northeast to Thrace, the Gallipoli Peninsula, and the Black Sea. Most Greek colonists remained close to the coast and dealt amicably with the local population. But when they had to, they were prepared to fight the native inhabitants. Although the Greek colonists may have set out with the most peaceable intentions, they often arrived in a spirit of conquest, usurping the lands and resources of other peoples just as their Greek and Ionian ancestors had done.

The Greeks brought their own culture with them to the colonies, but they were also receptive to the ways of the local inhabitants. As these borrowed skills and customs drifted back to Greece, they became tinged with the style the Greeks infused in everything they touched. In this way, the Greek colonists eventually adopted new and more advanced techniques and motifs in pottery, sculpture, and architecture. But more important, the Greeks acquired two practices that would revolutionize not only their own society

*Above, a painting of ca. 525 B.C. on a pinax, or wooden panel, showing a group preparing to sacrifice a sheep. The life of the ancient Greeks was permeated by religion, not so much in the form of creed or theology as in the desire to observe rituals such as this. The simple lyre and double-reed flute indicate the large part music played in ceremonial life.*

but all civilizations to come—the alphabet and coinage. Both had Asian origins, the alphabet coming from the Phoenicians and coins from the Lydians, inhabitants of Asia Minor.

Writing became fairly widespread in Greece by the late eighth century B.C., while the first coins were struck by the middle of the seventh century, an innovation that was soundly opposed by the more conservative Greek cities. The leaders of these cities had begun to recognize what to us is commonplace: that commerce would bring unsettling change as well as increased opportunity.

As the Greeks began to move beyond a subsistence-and-barter economy, land was no longer the prime gauge of wealth and inheritance no longer the main route to power. In addition, a new political structure, called the *polis,* began to dominate the local governments. Polis, which literally means city, actually denoted the state and the citizens who formed that state. Each polis, or city-state, was identified historically with a tribe.

Although the city-state is typically recognized as the forerunner of democracy, the opportunities to participate in managing the early polis were unequally distributed. Large numbers were absolutely forbidden from citizenship—women, slaves, foreigners, among others. More important, the old-guard aristocracy was reluctant to share power with the general citizenry. By 650 B.C., tensions stemming from failures in the organization of the city-states introduced a new phenomenon, the tyrant.

The term "tyrant"—or *tyrannos*—was originally intended to distinguish between those who usurped power and hereditary kings, and did not have a negative connotation. Tyrants were often members of the polis who bypassed both the aristocracy and the constitution and assumed powers greater than those traditionally allowed. Because they relied on the support of the people in claiming absolute authority, tyrants were generally regarded by the Greeks as undesirable effects of overly democratic city-states.

Tyrants appeared in many guises. Pisistratus in Athens had a reputation for fairness. Others were corrupted by the possibilities of unchecked military authority. Although Herodotus and other historians of the era liked to assign suspicious and undesirable motives to the tyrants, they generally proved to be beneficial, providing strong leadership, dynamic foreign policies, and ambitious public works, in addition to promoting the cultural development of their city-states. In any case, the tyrant customarily acted as a broker in the transfer of power from the more autocratic establishment to the newly emergent democratic forces.

One polis that never saw the need for a tyrant but which among all the city-states we might be most inclined to label autocratic was Sparta. Located in southern Peloponnesus, Sparta had been a major center of the Dorians ever since they imposed their rule over five villages in the area known as Laconia. Between 740 and 720 B.C., they conquered the region of Messenia to the west. When the Messenians revolted some eighty years later, the Spartans reduced

*The stone tripod incised with geometric designs (left) was used for sacrifices, an essential element of the Greeks' religion based upon the belief that the gods had the same need for food and drink as did men. Above, a painted terra-cotta metope from the sixth-century B.C. Temple of Apollo at Thermum. It depicts a daughter of Pandion, mythical king of prehistoric Athens, making a sacrifice.*

senian conquest. The Spartans, for instance, officially rejected the new silver and gold coinage and retained their own iron bar currency, thus deliberately isolating themselves from the new world of international trade. Indeed, they showed little interest in commerce or travel and often forcibly expelled foreigners from their domain.

In keeping with its respect for discipline and obedience, Sparta subjected its people to military exercises and civic obligations, as if it were in a permanent state of siege. The helots and other lower classes had few rights and were obligated to supply food for the elite upper class, the *spartiates,* or full citizens. Young spartiates were taken from their families at the age of seven and raised in barracks until they were thirty. There they underwent demanding physical training. One of their "festivals," for example, required youths to run a gauntlet of whip-wielding men and to remove a small ceremonial cake from an altar.

All youths went barefoot, ate simple food, and slept on mats of rushes. They were educated only in the military and political arts—artistic expression was not encouraged. At the age of twenty, each youth was nominated to join one of the all-male messes, or dining clubs, and at thirty he became a full citizen with the privilege of attending the Apella.

Sparta was equipped with a professional army at a time when other city-states were usually defended by temporary militias or mercenaries. As a result, Sparta had far more impact on Greek political history than its small population or meager financial resources would otherwise have warranted. Since the Spartan ideal was stability—and disorder their greatest fear—the army was valued not for imperial expansion but for preserving the status quo.

Sparta's dominion, secured with the defeat of Argos in 546 B.C., was limited to the Peloponnesian peninsula. Sparta ruled the area by forming military alliances and treaties with several other city-states of

them to the status of *helots*—serfs who were required to turn over half the produce of their labors to their Spartan masters. Other residents of Laconia ruled by the Spartans were called the *perioeci,* or "dwellers-around." Although they were free citizens and could be drafted into military service, they had no political rights in the Spartan state.

The strict organization of the Spartan government was, according to legend, an outcome of the reforms of Lycurgus, prior to Sparta's dominance of Laconia. At the top of the hierarchy were five overseers, or *ephors,* who were elected annually, and a council of elders, or Gerousia, which effectively ruled Sparta. The Spartans also had two kings, who planned and commanded military operations—a crucial task—and performed religious ceremonies—a less significant responsibility. An assembly of equals, the Apella, was composed of citizens over thirty who served as a channel for public opinion.

Although the traditional image of Sparta—rigid and conservative—is an oversimplification, it is true that the Spartans had a long tradition of authoritarianism. Many historians would trace Sparta's rigid ways to the need to suppress its growing population of helots, but the Spartan preference for hard work and demanding conditions was present before the Mes-

*A silver tetradrachma of ca. 550 B.C. (above left), an example of Athens' early adaptation of coinage, shows the head of Athena. Images of Greek life include (facing page, top to bottom): a boar hunt, from the François vase of ca. 570 B.C.; youths exercising at a palestra, or exercise field, from a red-figured vase painting; and a two-horse chariot race, from an embossed bronze belt. Following pages, Sparta today, with but a few ruins to attest to this once powerful rival of Athens.*

Certain deities were worshiped throughout the Greek world and among these was Apollo. At Delphi the great altar at the Temple of Apollo (above) was dedicated by the island of Chios; the temple was approached by the Sacred Way (below). Corinth, which now boasts the only surviving sixth-century colonnade in Greece, erected a temple to Apollo about 540 B.C. (left).

the Peloponnesus, all of whom were sufficiently intimidated by Sparta to risk rebellion or war. Thus, Spartan hegemony was based less on imperialistic ambition than on an unwavering commitment to security. It was this ingrained resistance to expansion that distinguished Sparta from Athens and eventually brought the two city-states into armed conflict.

A historian of the ancient world wrote that "Attica, since time immemorial, has been inhabited by the same race of people." This observation—recorded by the Athenian Thucydides—suggests the pride with which the Athenians viewed their Ionian heritage. A Mycenaean center, Athens survived the Dorian invasions, giving its people reason to consider themselves better, or "purer," than their Dorian neighbors. In fact, Athens prospered during the centuries when most of the Greek world was shrouded in the dark ages.

With the dawn of the Greek awakening, however, Athens was both commercially and culturally overshadowed by the accomplishments of several more progressive city-states, including Corinth and eastern Ionia. Only in its form of government did Athens show signs of precocious development.

Having abolished its hereditary monarchy early, by 683 B.C., Athens allowed its citizens—an elite group of adult males—to elect the chief rulers, the nine *archons*. Predictably, the aristocratic families stubbornly held onto as much power as they could, resulting in deep social tensions. When the plight of the peasantry

was further worsened by the outbreak of war with Megara, in 621 B.C., Athens elected Draco as special commissioner to codify existing law and alleviate the tensions between the rich and poor. Draco introduced such severe reforms that his name became synonymous with inflexibility even among the ancients. He nonetheless deserves credit for requiring that all cases of homicide be decided in the courts. Formerly, homicide had been considered a private affair and was settled by family vendettas.

Though far-reaching, Draco's laws favored the wealthy landowners and did little to curb the mounting economic and social unrest in Attica. The introduction of money had been forcing small landholders and the poor deeper and deeper in debt: Where formerly they had relied on a system of barter, they were now required to seek credit with cash. The poor had their land to offer as security, but if they fell behind on loan payments, even that was taken from them. Having relinquished their land, the poor were forced to offer themselves or their families into servitude. In this way, many landless freemen consigned themselves to slavery. Meanwhile, those with property or money were becoming wealthier still. The situation was so explosive that, within a generation of Draco's laws, the Athenians saw the necessity for additional reforms.

About 594 B.C., they elected as archon a man who had the reputation of being just and impartial, and they invested him with unprecedented legislative power. His name was Solon, and although of noble

# The gods of Olympus

Plato, in the *Epinomis,* noted that: "We may take it that whatever the Greeks inherit from other races, in the end they turn it into something better." The Olympian gods were inherited from a number of sources, both Mediterranean and Near Eastern. Ritual practices among the Greeks varied but a fairly coherent body of mythology developed about the main Olympian deities. This mythology was based on Homer's writings, from which the Greeks took their understanding of the gods.

Zeus ruled the weather and sky. Poseidon was lord of the sea, Hades of the underworld. Apollo guided the sun and supervised poetry and music. Hephaestus was god of the forge, Hermes of messages and boundaries. Hera ruled over women, Athena over wisdom, Aphrodite over love and beauty.

Although the cult of Dionysus, god of wine and fertility, dominated later Greek worship, Greeks honored the many gods long into their history, passing their polytheism on to the pre-Christian Romans.

*Above, Mount Olympus, the highest mountain (9,550 feet) in Greece, regarded as the dwelling place of Zeus and his family of gods. On the pediment (left) of the Temple of Artemis at Corfu, ca. 575 B.C., Zeus battles with a giant who has ambushed him, but often "the father of men and gods" was portrayed as more divine and Olympian.*

*A tribute to the widespread appeal of the Greek deities is this Roman statue (right) of Venus Genetrix, the Greek's Aphrodite, goddess of love. Another popular Greek deity was Dionysus, god of wine, depicted on an Attic amphora (facing page, below left), ca. 520 B.C. Appropriately, Dionysus is enwrapped in a grapevine and holds a wine kantharos.*

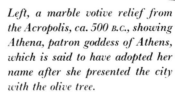

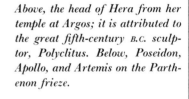

*Left, a marble votive relief from the Acropolis, ca. 500 B.C., showing Athena, patron goddess of Athens, which is said to have adopted her name after she presented the city with the olive tree.*

*Above, the head of Hera from her temple at Argos; it is attributed to the great fifth-century B.C. sculptor, Polyclitus. Below, Poseidon, Apollo, and Artemis on the Parthenon frieze.*

# Athenian democracy

"The will of no single person rules this land. It is a free city. The whole people, year by year, in equal service, is our ruler." So boasted a character in *The Suppliants* of Euripides. But when the citizens were called to assemble at the basic democratic forum, the Ecclesia, many Athenians were denied "equal service."

Women, slaves, and resident aliens did not enjoy the rights of citizenship. At Athens' peak in the fifth century B.C., only a small proportion of the populace were true citizens, and many of them were too busy, poor, or far away to attend the Ecclesia. The Ecclesia met approximately once a week on the Pnyx, the slope facing the Acropolis, in an open-air auditorium. The orator's stand was cut out of the natural rock at one side, and behind this sat fifty members of the council, or Boule.

Following the reforms of Cleisthenes in the late sixth century B.C., the Boule was composed of fifty representatives from each of the ten "tribes" of Athens, and these five hundred acted as a control board. No business could be discussed by the Ecclesia unless it had first been considered and proposed by the Boule.

Athens' democracy, then, was limited, at best, and gave rise to many idiosyncratic practices. Several influential offices, for example, were supposedly assigned by lot, yet members of old wealthy families habitually managed to get reelected. Another peculiarity was ostracism, a secret vote used by Athenians to exile political undesirables. The names of candidates were scratched into *ostraca* (above), broken pieces of pottery.

*The metal discs (left) were inserted into tally boards, or kleroteria, by Athenian citizens serving on trial juries. Discs with solid hubs indicated a vote of "not guilty," while discs with hollow hubs indicated a finding of "guilty."*

descent he was not wealthy. As were all early Greek men of letters, he was a poet and was well acquainted with the progressive cultural life of Ionia, a knowledge he would apply when he formulated his reforms for Athens. Undoubtedly, too, he knew enough to marshall the advice and support of prominent individuals in Athens' ruling class, without whom he could not have gone far.

Solon's first act was to restore freedom or land to those who had lost them paying their debts. He then converted the monetary system of Athens from the standard of the island of Aegina to the currency issued by Corinth. The new coins had slightly less silver, allowing debtors to pay in a cheaper currency. More important, this new monetary system moved Athens from the restricted economic sphere of Aegina into the more dynamic international market led by Corinth.

Solon also prohibited the export of cereal grains from Attica and promoted the cultivation of olives. He undertook this reform because the soil of Attica was more conducive to growing olives than grains, but in the long run the change made Athens dependent on importing grains. To enforce this new, more progressive commercial economy, Solon recommended that every young Athenian be trained in a specific trade. He also granted citizenship to craftsmen and tradesmen who settled in Athens, thus encouraging a healthy influx of skilled labor.

It was Solon's constitutional and political reforms that gained him the reputation as founder of Athenian democracy. Previously, Athens had been divided into three classes, with the landed aristocracy effectively controlling the offices of government. Solon now divided the free citizens into four classes with membership assigned according to the amount of produce yielded by each person's land. Although land remained the basis of citizenship, the amount required for this privilege was relatively modest. Furthermore, citizens of all four classes now belonged to the assembly, or *ecclesia,* which gave them the right to vote on laws, determine matters of war and peace, and elect officials. The courts, or *heliaea,* were also made up of men, thirty years and over, from the four classes, so that all citizens could look to them to administer justice.

As much power as Solon's reforms gave the common people, Athens' government was still far from a democracy. Only members of the two highest classes could become archons, and only archons could become members of the supreme council, the Areopagus. Prior to Solon's reforms, the Areopagus apparently discussed all matters before they reached the assembly, thus limiting the assembly's initiative.

The hill of Areopagus (above), across from the Acropolis, gave its name to the council of nobles that met there. Once the most influential governing body of Athens, the Areopagus gradually lost its powers, beginning with the reforms introduced by the legislator Solon (left) about 594 B.C. But beyond institutions, legislators, and even laws, much of Athenian democracy depended upon informal meetings at the Agora, or main market, and in the tholos, or circular structure (below).

Solon divested the Areopagus of this prerogative and granted it the role of protector of the constitution and guardian of the laws. Although its specific functions remained undefined, it can be said that the Areopagus effectively served as a conservative force by virtue of its aristocratic membership.

Solon created a more democratic council, or *boule*, to review matters of state before they reached the assembly. This council was composed of four hundred men chosen by lot, one hundred from each of the four tribes. Although the boule was only a part of the organization of the assembly, its function of preparing the agenda for the larger body gave it an important status in the Athenian state.

Solon's reforms left the upper classes with many of the reins of power, thus inviting criticism from the more popular minded. His enfranchisement of the poor, on the other hand, drew fire from the more traditional elements. To take refuge from his critics, Solon went into voluntary exile for several years after effecting his reforms. Tensions flared up shortly after his departure, polarizing around two parties: that of "the plains," the landed aristocracy who wanted to hold onto their age-old privileges and that of "the coast," the fishermen and city craftsmen who wanted to promote Solon's reforms on behalf of the newly enfranchised population. Pisistratus, a hero of renewed battle with Megara, led a third party, that of "the hills," composed of all those who could not identify with the extremes of the other two. Claiming to have been injured in Athens by his enemies, Pisistratus was assigned a bodyguard of fifty clubmen with whom he seized the Acropolis and took control of Athens. Eventually exiled, Pisistratus attempted a second ruse before a third one finally landed him the office of tyrant of Athens in 560 B.C. His dubious contribution to the art of seizing power was to have used mercenaries as well as support from foreigners opposed to Athens.

*Although the political and cultural affairs of the city-states attracted and still attract much interest and study, agriculture was the principal activity of most Greeks, and its memory is well preserved in decorative art. The relief (above far left) shows a woman picking quinces, a favorite fruit, while the bowl (above left) was made to hold fruit. The black-figured vase painting (left) shows farmers plowing with a team of oxen, while a man breaks up the soil with a pickax. Above right, a vase painting depicting a vineyard scene, and another vase (right) showing women picking fruit.*

# Food and drink

The diet of the ancient Greeks varied over the centuries and from place to place, but at all times their staple foods were fish and cereal grains.

Rising early, Greeks of all classes ate a bit of bread, possibly dipped in wine. About noon, they ate a modest meal, usually including fish. The word *opson*, which originally meant anything that was eaten with bread, came to refer exclusively to fish. The only full meal came near sunset, but even then the poor seldom ate meat. The one exception was pork, which was valued as a digestive. Otherwise, meat was a rarity, destined for the tables of the wealthy or for consumption on feast days.

Few Greeks drank milk or ate many eggs, but everyone enjoyed goats' cheese and used olive oil generously. To sweeten foods, they used honey—sugar was unknown. As for drink, the Greeks enjoyed wine, but never drank it straight, preferring to dilute it with water (usually two parts of wine to three of water).

Above all, Greeks valued moderation in eating and drinking, as in all things. Together, moderation and exercise were necessary for achieving the enviable "sound mind in a sound body."

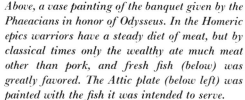

*Above, a vase painting of the banquet given by the Phaeacians in honor of Odysseus. In the Homeric epics warriors have a steady diet of meat, but by classical times only the wealthy ate much meat other than pork, and fresh fish (below) was greatly favored. The Attic plate (below left) was painted with the fish it was intended to serve.*

*Two mainstays of the Greek diet were olives (top) and grapes (above). Both the olive tree and the grapevine grew wild in Greece; their cultivation, probably introduced from Asia Minor or the Middle East, was begun by 3000 B.C.*

*Fruit was greatly enjoyed by the Greeks and a selection is memorialized (right) in a terra-cotta work from Rhodes. Quinces, apples, pears, and plums were common, and apricots and peaches were prized. There were no citrus fruits, but the Greeks ate many figs (below), fresh and dried. Fig trees provide two or more crops a year.*

# Women

Greek society left little room for participation by women. They could not vote—even in Athens—and their property was disposed of either by a husband or by the closest male relative. In fact, women were not even considered worthy of love: The highest form of love was only of the spirit and only between men; heterosexual relations were tolerated only for the purpose of producing children. Further, even the most humane and just Greek rulers considered women unfit for the affairs of state. As Aristotle observed: "The slave has no will; the child does have one, but it's incomplete—the woman also, but it's impotent."

Despite social and legal disenfranchisement, women were hardly slaves. They played a prominent role in things domestic, and may even have managed some political influence: In one of his satires, Aristophanes describes a revolution by the women of Athens, who used sexual politics to force a settlement of the Peloponnesian War. In addition, the portrayal of strong women in Sophocles' *Antigone* and *Electra* as well as the universal respect for Sappho, a poetess who lived on the island of Lesbos, show that the Greeks could not afford to ignore the role of women in society.

*Left, a woman painted on a lekythos, ca. 440 B.C., wearing the typical clothing of the time. Over her full-length tunic, or* chiton, *she wears a heavier, probably woolen, dark mantle, or himation. The elegant dipper, or* kyathos *(right), also from ca. 450 B.C., was used for pouring balms or unguents.*

*The two women (below), painted on a vase from southern Italy, have dropped their mantles and exposed their filmy tunics as they relax alone on a warm day. Widely used in the hot and sunny climate were the parasols made of cloth stretched over wooden ribs and the fan made of thin wood.*

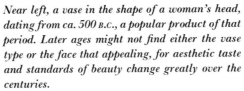

Near left, a vase in the shape of a woman's head, dating from ca. 500 B.C., a popular product of that period. Later ages might not find either the vase type or the face that appealing, for aesthetic taste and standards of beauty change greatly over the centuries.

The bronze vessel (far left), ca. 450 B.C., was used to hold perfumes or incense. The Greeks, like many peoples of the ancient world, did not bathe too often, and men as well as women commonly used various perfumes, unguents, and oils. Beyond that, the world of the ancients was pervaded with odors, from those of animals and fires to burning incense.

Right, a statue of a maiden, ca. sixth century B.C., of the traditional type known as a kore. She wears the full-length chiton, and over it the peplos, a waist-length mantle. This ensemble expresses the Greek ideal of feminine dress—elegance, simplicity, freedom, and modesty, for women were expected to keep their bodies, including their legs, well covered in public.

*Above, a famed funerary stele, ca. 400 B.C., from a cemetery in Athens. It portrays Hegeso selecting jewelry from a box held by her servant. The scene from a Corinthian krater (above right), ca. 560 B.C., shows a newly married couple about to depart in a chariot.*

*Two vase paintings show Greek women involved in domestic chores and athletic activity— right, a woman washing her hair, and far right, women racing. The Athenian coin (center right) uses two symbols of Athena, the owl and the olive.*

Once in control, Pisistratus instituted several populist reforms—for example, expropriating land from his defeated enemies and distributing it among the peasantry, and sending justices of the peace throughout Attica to allow farmers direct access to the courts. He also loaned farmers money from his own mines on Thrace and made himself available to anyone with a complaint. Like tyrants before him, Pisistratus was a man of the people—he knew the power of the appeal to the common classes. At the same time, he controlled all official bodies of the government, saw that offices were assumed by friends and supporters, and acted as the final arbiter in matters of state expendi-

tures. To underline his authority, he held the Acropolis as a private citadel and maintained his own mercenary force.

Economically, Pisistratus raised Athens above the other Greek city-states. He encouraged the production of olive oil and wine, two valuable export products. Pisistratus also coined new money with the two symbols of Athens—the sacred owl of the Acropolis on one side and the goddess Athena on the other. This silver money became the reserve currency of international trade, its success complementing Pisistratus' foreign policy, which combined a strict regard for peace with other Greek powers with a measured im-

perialism at the edges of the non-Greek world.

Pisistratus conducted other programs aimed at improving the quality of Athenian life. He supported new civic projects, such as the development of a city water supply. He also promoted a sense of Athenian community and encouraged the arts. Pisistratus was responsible for introducing Homeric epics to the Panathenaean festival, held in celebration of the unification of Attica.

Perhaps his greatest contribution to Athenian arts was his promulgation of the cult of Dionysus, god of wine and fertility. Under Pisistratus, the Athenians organized a new festival called the Great Dionysia of the City. One attraction of the event was the "goat song," sung by a choir of satyrs (Dionysus' attendants) dressed in goat skins. This performance eventually came to involve the recitation of a story. Two or more choirs would compete to sing the best story and tell the best tale in a so-called "tragic" contest. With the addition of actors to dramatize the stories, these contests began to assume the form of the Greek tragedies we recognize today.

Pisistratus, despised by later Greeks as a tyrant but

former supporters, and subsequently disenfranchised many citizens. The Alcmaeonids, led by Cleisthenes, responded by promising to return these rights and to institute reforms even more democratic than those of Solon. Cleisthenes gained the upper hand by drawing on the support of a host of poor noncitizens, and Isagoras had no choice but to call on the Spartans for help, who sent a small band of soldiers to Athens. But the Athenians, putting aside their various party affiliations, forced Isagoras and the Spartans to leave.

*Near right, Roman copies of the statues of Aristogiton and Harmodius, who killed the Athenian tyrant Hipparchus in 514 B.C. Although their motives were personal, they were hailed as heroes of democracy and honored with statues in the Agora. Among the Ionian Greeks who anticipated the classical achievements were Thales of Miletus (above far right), one of the Seven Sages, and Sappho the poetess (below right), depicted with Alcaeus, another poet from Lesbos, on a vase from the fifth century B.C.*

*The telesterion at Eleusis (left) was the site of initiations into the mystery cult of Demeter. Below, Aesop and a fox, depicted on an Attic vase. Said to have been a slave from Samos, but perhaps a mythical figure, Aesop was credited with writing most Greek fables.*

considered a benevolent dictator by the more charitable evaluation of later historians, passed the reins of government on to his two sons, Hippias and Hipparchus. The younger, Hipparchus, was assassinated in an unsuccessful revolt led by the famed "tyrannicides," Harmodius and Aristogiton. Hippias, who had been governing with a firm but prudent hand, became a harsh, suspicious ruler in response to the revolt. As the Athenians became increasingly disaffected, the Alcmaeonids, a noble Athenian family, seized the opportunity for a coup. They enlisted the aid of the Spartans—ever wary of tyrants. In 510 B.C., the Peloponnesian League attacked Athens, forcing Hippias and Pisistratus' family into exile. Sparta withdrew its forces from Athens, but not before obliging Athens to join the Peloponnesian League.

The conservative Isagoras won the chief archonship in 508 B.C., with the backing of Pisistratus'

After a long exile, the Alcmaeonids finally returned to Athens in power.

The reforms that followed are attributed to Cleisthenes. The old assemblies remained—the Areopagus, the Boule (although this was enlarged from four to five hundred members), the Ecclesia, the Archons. But these institutions now became more accessible and responsive to a broader citizenry, loosening the monopoly of power formerly enjoyed by the old-guard families.

Cleisthenes was also responsible for dividing the city and Athenian countryside into three regions, which, in turn, were subdivided into ten groups called *trittyes*. He then organized ten tribes, each consisting of one trittye from each of the three regions. Cleisthenes also established the *deme*, equivalent to a neighborhood in a large city, as an independent political unit and based the political life of Athens on the tribes and demes. This arrangement undercut the traditional groupings that had always dominated the

political and economic spheres of Athens.

All those who belonged to the demes were entitled to attend the Ecclesia which nominated the men from whom the five hundred members of the Boule were chosen by lot. Executive power remained in the hands of the old aristocratic magistrates, the archons, but after 487 B.C., they too were selected by lot. Although members of the old aristocracy still tended to dominate the higher offices, the use of lots opened up the channels of power to others. The demes and tribes, taking the place of the old hereditary four tribes, also enabled men without royal blood to become leaders. Any Athenian citizen with the ambition and ability to succeed in politics was now free to do so, at least in theory.

The reforms attributed to Cleisthenes did not transform Athens overnight into a model of democracy, nor were they democratic in a modern sense. The ideological basis of the new government was *isonomia,* or "political equality," a practice which therefore excluded large groups of the population: women, slaves, and resident aliens. Even so, the

*This stele (far left) was placed over the grave of Aristion about 510 B.C. Life-size, of Pentelic marble, it was carved by Aristocles and is an idealization of the gentleman-warrior of the period. His armor was made of leather, rather than metal, and Aristion looks like a man born to command, rather than to engage in bloody combat.*

*Left, a Corinthian helmet of the kind worn by heavily armed Greek hoplites at the time they were fighting the Persians and Medes, shown carved in relief (right) at the Persian capital of Persepolis. Armed with shields, the Persians appear a formidable enemy, yet they fell before the hoplites.*

Athenian government of about 500 B.C. was the most ambitious attempt yet made by a city-state to involve a large number of its people in the governing process. The Athenians, in fact, had experimented more with politics in three centuries than all other ancient peoples had done in three thousand years. But the future of that experiment was now threatened by the advances of the Persians under Darius the Great.

For some five hundred years the Greeks had relatively few disputes or open conflicts with foreigners. Occasionally, small groups of Greeks had fought with outsiders, usually because the Greeks intruded on alien territory. But never had the entire Greek world been pitted against a common enemy.

During those five centuries the Greeks, for all their domestic squabbling, had created a consciously Greek culture. The works of Homer and Hesiod had transformed their myths, legends, and history into a legacy that spoke to all Greeks. The Olympic games, instituted in 776 B.C., did more than any other institution to subdue the chronic devisiveness of the Greeks by providing a Panhellenic link that was to prove stronger than the running feuds and strains among the city-states.

Even so, factionalism was as recognizably Greek as the emerging Panhellenic consciousness. "Strife is wholesome to men," wrote Hesiod, and for centuries the interplay of culture and conflict had worked to produce a people who learned to coexist in a state of mutual respect and distrust. The Athenians and the Spartans could afford to disagree because no great foreign power had threatened them during the crucial formative centuries of their civilization. The approach of a new empire—that of the Persians—brought this climate of friendly rivalry to an end in the sixth century B.C.

The Ionian Greeks were the first to seek support in their struggle against Persia, the most powerful state of the time. Since 547 B.C. the Ionian city-states along the coast of Asia Minor had been under the rule of the Persians, whose government and culture were fundamentally different from those of the Greeks. The Persians ruled their growing empire with a relatively light hand. Allowing the Ionians, for instance, to keep their own language, religion, and customs, the Persians placed their own overlords in control of the city-states and required the Greeks to provide both tribute and taxes. However, the highly centralized Persian state, which demanded absolute devotion to its king, was a continuous imposition on the traditionally self-ruled Ionian Greeks—as were the taxes. When the situation became intolerable in 499 B.C., some of the more disgruntled revolted, appealing for assistance from the cities of their motherland.

Characteristically, the Spartans refused to be drawn into such an obviously volatile situation. But Athens and Eretria, a city-state on Euboea, sent a total of twenty-five ships. Vastly overpowered, the Ionians lost the important naval battle of Lade in 494 B.C. after several early successes. A year later the polis that led the Ionian revolt, Miletus, was destroyed and its women and children deported to Mesopotamia. By 493 B.C., the rebellion was crushed.

The Persian king appointed tyrants to suppress the Ionians and discourage further insurrection. Typically, the Persians soon moderated this policy, replacing the tyrants with more democratic governments. The Persians could afford to be tolerant toward the Ionians, but they were naturally wary of the Athenians, whose ambitions challenged Persia's own commercial and territorial aspirations in the Mediterranean area.

The Persian king, Darius I, ordered a land expedition to march around the northern coast of the Aegean through Thrace and Macedonia and, finally, into Greece. The Persian land force, in league with the support of a fleet sailing along the coast, subdued Thrace, Macedonia, and the island of Thasos in 492 B.C. When a storm struck the fleet north of Greece, however, the expedition turned homeward, leaving Greece with more uneasiness than actual threat. Darius was not to be daunted. At the urging of the tyrant Hippias, who had gone into exile in Persia and nurtured ambitions to rule Athens, Darius launched a fleet across the Aegean in the summer of 490 B.C. The Greeks later spoke of the Persian force as countless, but it probably numbered no more than 25,000 infantrymen at the most.

Naturally, having never faced a major foreign invasion, Athens dreaded the approach of the Persian fleet. But under the leadership of the general Miltiades, who had once served under Darius, Athens formed an alliance with Eretria and Sparta—Athens' determined foe less than twenty years earlier. The Persians landed at Euboea and placed the city of Eretria under siege, which proved an easy target. Having entrenched themselves at Eretria, the Per-

*The Persian invasion of 490 B.C. was launched by King Darius (above far right), carved in relief at Persepolis. Miltiades (above center right), an Athenian noble, organized the Greek resistance. After defeating the Persians at Marathon, the Greeks buried their 192 dead on the plain and raised a thirty-foot high mound over them (top left).*

*At the base of the burial mound at Marathon, the Greeks erected a stele (center left). Known as "the Warrior of Marathon," it had actually been carved in 510 B.C. Then, at Delphi, the Athenians erected a treasury (right). Inside they placed a plaque (bottom left) inscribed: "The Athenians dedicate to Apollo the spoils of the Medes after the battle of Marathon."*

125

# Greek vases

A pot is a container made beautiful because the potter's wheel enforces symmetry. The Greeks enhanced this beauty with paintings that are almost the only remnants of Greek two-dimensional art.

The shape of the Greek pot reflects its function. Wine was mixed with water in the krater and drunk from the kylix, skyphos, and kantharos. The psykter kept wine cool while the narrow-necked lebes, amphora, pelike, and stamnos were easily sealed for storing wine. Perfume and oil were measured from the aryballos and lekythos. The hydria held water.

Corinthian craftsmen made the first advance in pottery, perfecting their art while the rest of the Greek world slept through the pre-eighth century B.C. "dark ages." But by the fifth century, Athenian workshops had inherited Corinth's reputation for producing the finest clay wares.

*The volute krater (above) was used for mixing wine and water. The lekythos (left) was designed for easy pouring of oil or other liquids and was used especially for offerings to the dead. The pelike (below), with its painting of a vase vendor, was used for holding wine.*

*Above, two vases adorned with human heads, used for drinking wine on special occasions. The amphora (below), one of the most familiar shapes of Greek vases, was actually awarded as a prize at the Panathenaean games in the event depicted—the discus throw.*

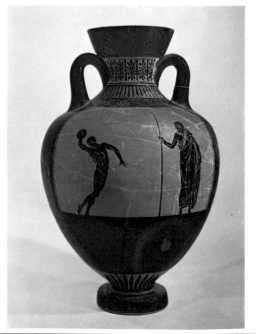

The oinochoe (above) was a jug or decanter for pouring liquids. The kantharos (left) was used for drinking wine. The small krater (below left) is decorated with a scene involving Hermes. The rhyton (below) has a hole in the mouth of the ram's head; a person was expected to hold a finger over the hole and then, when ready to drink, raise the rhyton and let the wine arch into his mouth.

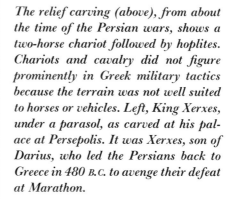

*The relief carving (above), from about the time of the Persian wars, shows a two-horse chariot followed by hoplites. Chariots and cavalry did not figure prominently in Greek military tactics because the terrain was not well suited to horses or vehicles. Left, King Xerxes, under a parasol, as carved at his palace at Persepolis. It was Xerxes, son of Darius, who led the Persians back to Greece in 480 B.C. to avenge their defeat at Marathon.*

sians prepared to seek vengeance against Athens.

Despite Miltiades' early preparations, the Athenians had not yet mobilized their troops when they heard of Eretria's fall. Dispatching a runner, Pheidippides, to run the 150 miles between Athens and Sparta, the Athenian rulers hoped to enlist the support of the superbly trained Spartan troops. The Spartans, however, conveniently claimed to be caught up in a religious festival, but promised they would send troops when the full moon had passed. So the Athenians had no choice but to send 10,000 of their own troops to face the Persians on the plain of Marathon, just across from Euboea. By the time the Spartans arrived, the battle was over.

Far outnumbered by the Persians, the Greek troops set up a long, narrow center force on the plain, keeping strong wings in the hills where the Persian forces would be on rough, unfamiliar territory. All went as planned for Athens. The Persians easily pierced the Athenian center, but the Greeks destroyed the Per-

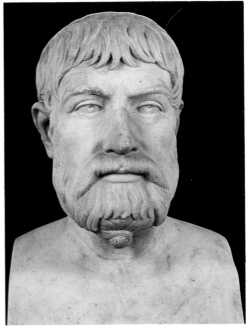

sian wings. The wing troops then moved down from the hills to enclose the Persian center, forcing the Persians to flee in total disarray. Fighting their way back to their ships, the Persians left behind seven ships and 6,400 dead soldiers. The Greeks counted their dead—192.

There was, however, little time to celebrate—the Persian host was still large enough to retaliate. After a forced march of some eight or nine hours, the Athenian troops arrived to see the Persian fleet nearing the coast the next morning. Incredulously, the soldiers watched as the Persians sailed past Athens and turned toward home, across the Aegean. It is not clear what convinced Darius that he should cancel the invasion. Perhaps he was intimidated by the sight of the Athenian defense or, more likely, he was aware of the Spartan force nearing the city. As it turned out, the Spartans arrived with nothing left to do but congratulate the Athenians.

Later ages would elevate the battle of Marathon into one of the great turning points in history, the day when Western civilization turned back Asian despotism. At the time, however, it was neither so dramatic nor so final. In fact, it was not the end of the Persian threat, but only one in a series of confrontations between the Greeks and the Persians that would continue for over two hundred years.

The Persians, determined to avenge their honor, spent the decade after Marathon preparing another campaign. In 480 B.C., they reappeared on the borders of Greece. An army of some 180,000 troops had marched around the Aegean through the lands conquered by the earlier Persian expedition of 492. In Thrace the troops were met by a fleet of 700 ships. From there the Persian generals plotted their final revenge.

During the same decade, Athens and the rest of Greece had not been idle. Athens sent out an expedition under Miltiades to attack the island of Paros, whose people had assisted Persia, but the siege proved unsuccessful. On returning to Athens, nursing a serious wound, Miltiades was condemned and fined by his critics, only to die soon thereafter.

He was succeeded by Themistocles, a member of a poor but aristocratic family. He was able to convince the Athenians that they should concentrate on building a navy, rather than relying, as was traditional, on their ground troops. The money for this project came from a recently discovered vein of silver, which had originally been earmarked for distribution among the citizenry. To rally public support for using the silver to finance the fleet, Themistocles prayed for an omen from the famous oracle at Delphi, to which Greeks often turned for advice. The oracle pronounced that only a "wooden wall" would be capable of resisting the Persians. Themistocles cleverly argued that this "wooden wall" was the oracle's designation for a fleet of wooden ships. The Athenian assembly approved Themistocles' interpretation—and the ship-building program—but not before he had ostracized his two chief opponents, Aristides and Xanthippus.

Themistocles also brought Sparta and several other city-states into an alliance to repel the Persians. Recognizing the danger to all of Greece, the Athenian leaders accepted Sparta's request to lead the alliance, which became known as the Greek League. Having united the Greek world in the face of the common threat, Athens resolved its domestic squabbles by recalling Aristides, Xanthippus, and other key statesmen who had been sent into exile. Greece was now prepared to meet the Persian challenge.

The Greeks planned on defending only the most vital parts of their homeland, discouraging the Persians by inflicting slow losses on their troops and dividing the opposing land force and navy. To halt the army, a force commanded by the Spartan Leonidas was sent to a narrow pass at Thermopylae, the only way the Persians could cross the mountains and march south to Attica. The Greek strategy was to stall the Persians at the pass until the sea battle was over. They were successful for several days until a man named Ephialtes betrayed his countrymen and led the Persians around a mountain path to the rear of the Greek army. Realizing that he was doomed, Leonidas dismissed all but three hundred of his own Spartan soldiers and seven hundred Thespians, all of whom—but two—were killed. The Spartans were typically stoical. When one Spartan observed that the Persian troops were so numerous that their arrows hid the sun, a fellow soldier was said to have replied: "So much the better, we will fight in the shade."

The Persians now moved south, but the Greeks quickly prepared a defense. The Athenians had no choice but to abandon their city according to plan, leaving it for the Persians, who set fire to its magnificent buildings, including those on the Acropolis. Meanwhile, the Greek fleet, headed by the Athenian *triremes* (galley ships with three tiers of oars) waited in the Bay of Salamis, just west of the Athenian port of Piraeus. One story claims that Themistocles sent a message to the Persian king Xerxes, who had accompanied his force, informing him that the Greek fleet

## Ostracism

Perhaps the most unusual institution that evolved with Athenian democracy was ostracism. It took its name from *ostraca*, broken pieces of pottery used to record votes. The practice is believed to have originated under Cleisthenes in the sixth century B.C., but its first recorded use was in 487 B.C.

Once a year the Ecclesia voted to determine whether to proceed with an *ostracaphoria*, a balloting with ostraca. If a majority voted affirmatively, a second vote was taken. Each citizen present was free to scratch onto an ostracon the name of a candidate for ostracism. If a majority of ballots bore the name of one man, he was consigned to a ten-year exile.

Ostracism started as a precaution against budding tyranny, but it was also a convenient means of settling political grudges or depriving minorities of leadership. Whatever its use, the practice did not imply irrevocable disgrace. In fact, many prominent Athenians, including Themistocles and Aristides, were targets of this system. Aristides, a political opponent of Themistocles, was ostracized only to return as a hero during Greece's second war with the Persians. He later became known as "Aristides the Just."

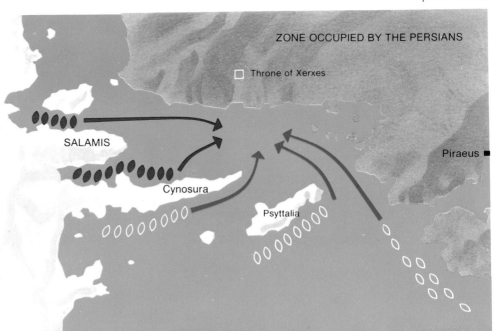

*Above, Themistocles, leader of the Athenian resistance against the second Persian invasion. He took steps to build a strong navy and was vindicated at the battle of Salamis in 480 B.C., illustrated (right) in its two main phases. Phoenician ships and sailors—shown on a Phoenician coin (below)—actually composed much of the Persian fleet.*

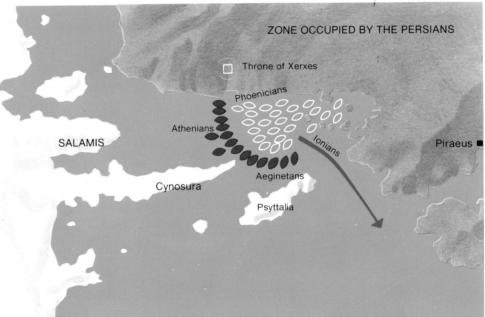

could be entrapped in the bay. According to the story, the message was intended to inspire the Persians to quick action, thereby forcing the indefatigably quarrelsome Greeks to unite against their common enemy. Whether or not the story is true, the Persian fleet obliged by advancing into the narrow bay on the morning of September 23, 480 B.C. The numerically superior Greek fleet outmaneuvered the enemy, and divided the unwielding Persian force. As Xerxes sat on a hill, confidently awaiting the end of the Greek resistance, some two hundred of his own ships were demolished and the remaining several hundred ships forced to flee.

Although the Greeks had not succeeded in crushing the Persians, the victory at Salamis would always be remembered as a decisive blow against the Persian navy. Several years later, the dramatist Aeschylus,

# Greek ships

The first Greek-speaking people evidently had so little experience with the sea that they borrowed its very name, *thalassa,* from earlier inhabitants. But after 800 B.C., the Greeks became the chief rivals of the Phoenicians for the honor of ruling the Mediterranean. The question of the superiority of Greeks or Phoenicians in ship design and invention remains uncertain.

By 850 B.C., the Greeks had added a pointed ram to the prow of warships, which suggests that they engaged in true naval battles, not just hand-to-hand combat among oarsmen aboard ship. By about 700 B.C., the two-banked galley came into use until it was outclassed in 550 B.C. by the faster, three-banked galley called the trireme. The Greek trireme could hold up to 170 oarsmen, and its battering ram—a lethal weapon—helped clear the seas for generations of Greek merchants. About 350 B.C., the Greeks returned to the single bank of oars, but with as many as four men on an oar. This proved so superior that subsequent ships added more and more men to each oar.

*Top left, a carving in natural rock at Lindos, Rhodes, of the stern of a ship with a seat for the helmsman. Originally, a statue of a priest stood on the deck. Center left, a terra-cotta model of a galley. The* penteconter, *or fifty-oared ship (bottom), was painted on a kylix by Exekias about 550 B.C. These grand warships used sails to cover long distances and oarsmen only to maneuver in combat or into harbors.*

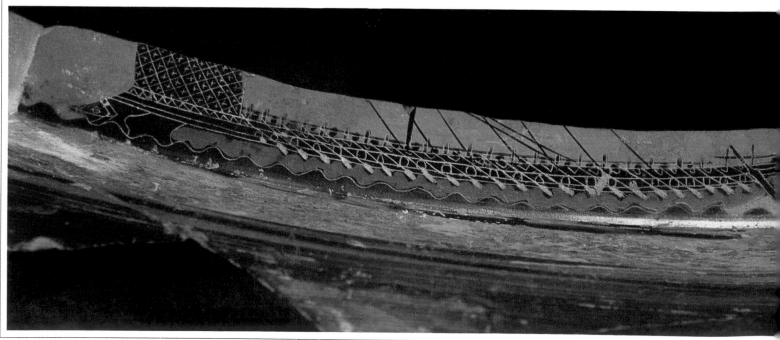

*Above, the prow of a ship on a coin issued by Antigonus II Gonatas, one of Alexander's successors. In the struggle for power that followed the death of Alexander, Antigonus and his family assumed leadership of Macedonia and, recognizing the new role of sea power, initiated a rivalry that led to the construction of some of the largest ships of antiquity.*

*In the detail (left) from one of the most famous of all Greek vase paintings—by Exekias, ca. 540 B.C.—Dionysus is shown in an episode from a Homeric hymn. Disguised as a youth, Dionysus was seized by pirates. Aboard their ship, he made a grapevine spring up around the mast; the terrified pirates jumped overboard and turned into dolphins. Dionysus then sailed on to Greece where he introduced the vine and his cult.*

*Right, a relief carving of an Athenian trireme, or three-banked warship—the kind used by Greeks at Salamis. It is not known who invented the trireme, but it was introduced by both Phoenicians and Greeks about 550 B.C. It is also somewhat uncertain how the oarsmen of the third bank were situated. The trireme was a smaller, sturdier, and more maneuverable ship than others in use at the time.*

# The age of individualism

No ancient civilization was more open to the efforts of the individual than that of Greece. Greek history is, in very large measure, a history of individual Greeks—their ambitions, convictions, successes, and tragedies.

The development of ancient Greece, especially that of Athens and Sparta, was in large part determined by a few outstanding individuals. The reforms of Solon, the leadership of Pericles, the treachery of Alcibiades stand out as prominent moments in Athenian history. Artists like Ictinus and Callicrates, who built the Parthenon, and Phidias, who designed its structure, made great contributions. The study of philosophy begins with Socrates, Plato, and Aristotle; history with Herodotus.

The Athenian democracy, based on the idea that individuals should share the responsibility of government, regardless of class distinction or political experience, gave the citizens considerably more room for development than did the Spartan aristocracy. Characteristically, the model Spartans are mainly soldiers, such as Leonidas and his nephew Pausanias.

Few Spartans became cultural leaders, since military prowess and rigid obedience to the state were valued over artistic development. Sparta's determined xenophobia further discouraged cultural exchange, so Athens was free to draw the finest minds from all over Greece. Although these Athenian residents could not become citizens, they made their adopted city the cultural and artistic center of the ancient world, one that has formed the basis for much of Western culture since antiquity.

*The Acropolis (below) had been a fortified citadel from the pre-Mycenaean period of Athens, but eventually it became a sanctuary of the gods. As such, the Acropolis was not the seat of civil government but the bulwark of Athens' spiritual ideals.*

## Xanthippus

Father of Pericles, Xanthippus played a key role in Athenian politics in the Persian wars. Ostracized in 484 B.C. by the faction led by Themistocles, Xanthippus returned to lead the Athenian fleet to victory over the Persians at Mycale in 479 B.C., an event that launched Athens as an imperial power.

## Pericles

Despite his aristocratic heritage, Pericles worked to broaden the democratic base of Athenian government. Beyond his political acts, it was his support of the arts that made Athens "the school of the Greeks." Yet Pericles was undeniably an imperialist: in one sense, he provoked the war with Sparta that led to the decline of Athens.

## Aspasia

A courtesan from Miletus, by 450 B.C., Aspasia was the mistress of Pericles. Aspasia was accused both of leading a scandalous life and of influencing Pericles' policies. But she was admired by the cultured circle surrounding Pericles and was one of few women to play a role in the public affairs of the golden age of Greece.

## Socrates

Born in 470 B.C., Socrates served as a soldier before settling down to become the gadfly of Athens. He was married to Xanthippe and they had three sons. Socrates evidently earned his living as a teacher, but he remained poor. He never wrote a line, and everything known about his teaching has come down to us through his disciples.

# Herodotus

A native of Halicarnassus in Asia Minor, Herodotus traveled widely throughout the ancient world. His history of the wars between the Greeks and the Persians provides an account of much of the known world. Although his work should be read critically, Herodotus is deservedly called "the father of history."

# Thucydides

Coming from an old Athenian family, Thucydides pursued a military career until he was exiled after failing in an expedition against the Spartans in 424 B.C. During the next twenty years he wrote a narrative of the wars between Athens and Sparta then in progress. Thucydides also analyzed the underlying causes of the war.

# Plato

Born into a great Athenian family, Plato became a student of Socrates. After Socrates' death, Plato went into self-imposed exile but soon returned to Athens to establish his Academy. His twenty-five dialogues that embody the work and person of Socrates as well as his own ideas are today a high point of Western thought.

# Pausanias

A Spartan general of royal descent, Pausanias led the Greek forces in their victory over the Persians at Plataea in 479 B.C. His personal ambitions, however, led to his being recalled, and he was accused of offering to enslave Greece for the hand of a Persian princess. He continued his intrigues and in 470 B.C. was condemned to death.

# Alcibiades

As a youth, Alcibiades had a promising future: Pericles was his guardian and Socrates his teacher. By 420 B.C., he assumed leadership of the more radical democrats, but he could not resist political intrigue. Accused of impiety, he deserted to Sparta and then to Persia. Alcibiades was assassinated in 406 B.C. by agents of Sparta and Athens.

# Lysias

Born to a Syracusan-Greek family, Lysias lived in Athens until the end of the war with Sparta, when he was exiled to nearby Megara. He continued to support democracy, however, and on returning to Athens, he became a speechwriter. His clear and simple style helped to elevate spoken Greek to the level of a literary language.

# Demosthenes

Orphaned at an early age, Demosthenes mastered law and rhetoric to regain the property his guardians had appropriated. (According to legend, he practiced speaking with pebbles in his mouth.) Demosthenes delivered a series of orations warning of the threat of Philip II. Ultimately abandoned by his own people, he committed suicide.

# Aeschines

The major political adversary of Demosthenes, Aeschines was apparently of humble origins but rose to prominence in Athenian public affairs. Sent in 348 B.C. with an embassy to Philip II, Aeschines returned convinced of the inevitability of the Macedonian takeover and thereafter attacked Demosthenes on both personal and political levels.

who had fought at Marathon and probably at Salamis, would commemorate the battle at Salamis as follows:

The Persian fleet, in a perpetual stream,
At first appeared invincible; but when
Their numbers in the narrows packed and
    hemmed
Grew dense, they cracked their oars in the tumult
And smote each other with their beaks of brass,
    and none could help their comrades.

After Salamis, the Persian army found itself trapped in a hostile land, with the sea at its back dominated by the Greeks. Xerxes left Attica, retreating north with his main force but leaving behind one corps to bargain with the Athenians. Its commander tried to divide the Greeks by offering the Athenians an alliance with Persia, but the Athenians refused. Instead, they mobilized one hundred thousand troops from the other Greek city-states, sending them against the Persians at Plataea, in central Greece. With Sparta's soldiers taking the lead, the Persians were solidly beaten and their remaining forces retreated from northern Greece. On the same day, Aristides led another Greek force that soundly de-

feated the Persians at Mycale, near Miletus, on the coast of Asia Minor.

The conflict with Persia was by no means ended, but for the moment the situation had been reversed. The Greeks had defeated the strongest military force of the day. The victory was costly. Ionia, once the most sophisticated and progressive region of Greece, had suffered a blow at the hands of the advancing Persians, from which it would never quite recover. Athens had been completely devastated by the Persian occupation. And these were only the more obvious costs. A more subtle price was to be paid by the Athenians as they now assumed their new role as leaders of the Greek world.

Although the Persian threat was still very much in evidence, even after the Greek's success at the battles of Plataea and Mycale, the Spartans were anxious to relinquish the leadership of the Greek League. Indeed, Sparta balked at the obligation to support any further international involvements. The weaker Greek city-states then turned to Athens, for its fleet had emerged as the most spectacular new instrument of Greek power. Athens was not reluctant to accept the Spartans' old role, and in 478–477 B.C., a new confederation was formed.

This alliance, called the Delian League, took its

*Right, a view of the great sanctuary on the island of Delos. A cult center from pre-Greek times, Delos remained a religious center over the ages as indicated by the temple (above), dedicated to the Egyptian goddess Isis and built by the Athenians in about 150 B.C.*

name from the Aegean island of Delos, long a sacred spot to Greeks and now the site of the treasury and assembly of the league. All members of the Delian League were bound to Athens by individual treaties. Most important, each member accepted the condition that Athens would have as much power as all the other states combined, in return for which Athens would provide leadership. Some members were to contribute a designated number of properly equipped warships, while others were to contribute money. These and the many other terms of the coalition were determined by Themistocles and his former rival Aristides, who later became known as "the Just," for his statesmanship.

The Delian League was successful in its early years, driving the Persians out of Europe and freeing various Greek city-states in the east from the bondage of the Persians. The league's most glorious moment came in 467 B.C., when the Athenians under Cimon, son of Miltiades, led the Greeks to victory over the Persians at the Eurymedon River in Asia Minor.

With Athens' authority over the Delian League came a new Athenian attitude toward diplomacy and conquest. The Greeks had long exerted military force,

*The restored columns of the Temple of Poseidon (right) at Cape Sounion are in the Doric order but are unusual in having sixteen flutes instead of twenty. The foundation dates from an earlier temple, and some of its columns were used when this temple was erected around 444 B.C. to become a familiar landmark to ships on the Aegean.*

# Athletics

Homer gives the earliest description of the Greek athletic games. His vivid description of the funeral games of Patroclus in the *Iliad* shows the ritual importance of athletics. Hesiod, writing in the eighth century B.C., relates that people traveled fifty kilometers or more to attend funeral games, a great distance for the time. And the *Hymn to Apollo,* attributed to Homer, glorified the games held on Delos in honor of Apollo, a festival which the Ionians attended "with their children and chaste wives."

The games were institutionalized, according to tradition, in 776 B.C. Olympia was designated as the site and a quadrennial schedule was established. The Olympic games were the most important, but there were others such as the Pythian games at Delphi, the Nemean, the Panathenaic, and the Isthmian.

Games were held in the summer, the most convenient time for traveling. Spectators and athletes arrived from every part of Hellas. Special truces among the Greek states suspended military operations for the period of the games to allow everyone access to them. Participants had to be Greek citizens. They received no monetary compensation—only wreaths or vases as prizes, along with enormous prestige and political favors.

The classic competitions were the races of various distances, the runners being nude or armed like hoplites; boxing; wrestling; the pancratium (which combined race, broad jump, discus throwing, javelin throwing, and wrestling); and the race with four-horse chariots.

*Among the many sports enjoyed by the Greeks was a kind of field hockey, depicted on the base of a statue (above) from the sixth century B.C. A black-figured vase painting (below) shows men boxing with leather thongs. Greek boxing did not involve rings, rounds, or weight classes. Another vase painting (right) shows the discus throw. Bronze replaced the stone discus in about 450 B.C.*

*Above, a black-figured painting of men racing, from an amphora awarded as prize for this event at the Panathenaean games. The unnatural stride is a standard artistic convention. Men competed naked, like the youth (left) pouring oil from an urn as he prepares to rub himself down to clean and condition his body before competing in the race.*

*The stadium at Delphi (center right), where the Pythian games were held, had a track some 582 feet long. Competitors in the Greek games were all amateurs except those in the four-horse chariot race (right), which was so dangerous and expensive that it required professional drivers and wealthy sponsors. Following pages, the Sanctuary of Olympia, with its stadium in the background.*

The Temple of Apollo at Aegina (above), with only one column left standing, was built about 510 B.C. Located in the Saronic Gulf off Attica, Aegina had a long-time commercial rivalry with Athens, which ended in 456 B.C. when Aegina was captured and recolonized by the Athenians.

Left, remains of the tholos at Epidaurus, a round structure of unknown function, part of the Sanctuary of Asclepius. The cult of this god of healing was originally local, but by 400 B.C., it was becoming Panhellenic and Epidaurus was becoming a place of pilgrimage. Epidaurus also sponsored a drama festival in its superb theater.

but the motives were usually more pragmatic—such as securing resources deemed necessary for survival—than openly imperialistic. The Athenians now began to exert power for the sake of their own advancement—but obstensibly in the interest of the Delian League. Athens forced Naxos, a city-state that had voluntarily left the league, to rejoin. The island of Scyros was simply seized, its inhabitants sold into slavery, and Athenian colonists assigned to the land, which now became a *cleruchy*. This new type of colony granted Athenian citizenship to its inhabitants, even though the colony was founded on foreign soil. Meanwhile, Cimon was forcing more and more members of the league to contribute money instead of ships. Athens funneled these funds into its own shipyards and assigned its own sailors to man the new ships. The Delian fleet was fast becoming the Athenian navy.

None of this was lost on the Spartans. Increasingly displeased with the emergent power of Athens, Sparta was constantly foiled in its efforts to restrict Athenian expansion, partly because of catastrophic problems at home. In 464 B.C., an earthquake devastated Sparta, leaving over 20,000 people dead. The helots and perioeci, many of them Messenians, seized this moment to revolt against Sparta, which had followed an unwise policy of subjugating—and therefore alienating—its slave population. Not yet Sparta's enemy, Athens joined several other city-states in sending troops to help Sparta suppress the rebellion. Athens' assistance did, however, come as a surprise to the Spartans.

This occasion was one of the last times these two city-states would cooperate albeit uneasily. Relations between them grew exceedingly complex and deteriorated quickly, finally erupting in 457 B.C., when the Athenian and Spartan forces met at Tanagra in central Greece. Although the Spartans won the battle, their losses were so heavy that they had no choice

*The tholos at Delphi (right) was erected about 390 B.C. Round temples became popular among Greeks in the fourth century B.C. Three of the twenty outer columns have been reerected. The dedication and purpose of this tholos remain unknown, but it lies within the Sanctuary of Athena Pronaia, which predated the Sanctuary of Apollo.*

143

# Greek mythology

Greek mythology links a disparate collection of religious beliefs, traditions, and customs. Mythology gave the Greeks a somewhat unruly national pantheon, one that allowed each city to honor its own patron deity and observe its own rituals. These myths not only told the stories of the gods themselves, who were often quite human despite their divine attributes, but also recounted the legends surrounding the Greek heroes.

Heroes were those select mortals who, through their semidivine lineage, could maintain their identity after death and escape the fate of common mortals, who were destined to be reduced to fleeting shadows. Such divine heroes—Heracles, Theseus, Perseus, and Achilles—moved men to acts of bravery and gave them courage.

Besides giving the Greeks a sense of community and a national conscience, myths were explanations for natural phenomena. The Greek mind was not so much interested in reasoning out the causes of natural processes as visualizing them in concrete terms. Lightning and storms, for

*The marble relief (right) shows Demeter, the goddess of agriculture, presenting a stalk of wheat to her son Triptolemus, behind whom stands Demeter's daughter, Persephone. Triptolemus spread the benefits of agriculture throughout the world. This relief, ca. 440 B.C., stood at Eleusis, home of the great Eleusinian mysteries, a cult of regeneration.*

example, were the province of Zeus, who habitually expressed his displeasure by throwing thunderbolts into the skies.

Some myths had no other purpose than to entertain. So it was that the myth maker would record the pain of disappointment in love, the futility of jealousy, or the consequences of ambition. In this respect, myth was literature, inspiring all Greeks with an image of what it is to be human.

The hero Heracles (below) is seen on a fragment of a vase painted by the great potter-painter Euphronius, active about 500 B.C. The myth of Heracles became one of the most popular throughout the Greek world.

A vase painting (above) shows Theseus being crowned by Athena as Poseidon looks on. Ariadne, whom Theseus abandoned after killing the Minotaur with her help, is shown marrying Dionysus.

Far left, a vase painting of Orpheus, the mythical singer who could charm animals and even stones. The cult of Orpheus became a religious movement, while the myth of Oedipus—depicted on a red-figured kylix (near left) as the sphinx proposes its riddle—inspired great tragedies.

This splendid kylix (right) depicts the Dioscuri, the inseparable twins Castor and Polydeuces (better known by his Latin name, Pollux). While Pollux was the son of Zeus, Castor was the son of a mortal; when Pollux refused immortality without Castor, Zeus transformed them into the constellation Gemini.

but to return home. Athens now became openly aggressive, forcing various city-states to accept the government it favored and subjugating any Greeks who presumed to resist Athenian policy. Athens also eradicated the last trace of the Delian League, which had become a mere façade. In 454 B.C., Athens transferred the league's money from the treasury at Delos to the Acropolis and subsequently closed the mints of its allies, who now had no choice but to adopt Athenian currency. With this decisive step, the league's governing body ceased to have any authority and no longer convened meetings.

Athens' Peace of Callias with Persia in 449 B.C., and the Thirty Years' Treaty with Sparta in 445 B.C., marked a pivotal moment in Athens' policy of aggression. In the treaties, Athens agreed to cease open hostilities with its two strongest rivals, surrendering its land empire to Sparta in exchange for Sparta's recognition of Athens' maritime supremacy. Athens was subdued, at least temporarily, but had made its entrance as an imperial power.

Along with Athens' political successes came a cultural awakening that would be known as the "golden age" of Athens. It was no coincidence that the construction of the Parthenon began at this time, in 447 B.C. The principal voice in the project was Pericles, who had played an important role in subjugating other Greek city-states. During the thirty years he was in politics, he was regularly elected to the highest office of general, the *strategos*. Pericles was almost universally respected for his breadth of views, his uncompromising commitment to the ideals of constitutional democracy, and his consummate ability to balance the forcefulness of a general with the skills of a politician. Pericles was also politically pure during a period noted for its morally corrupt Greek leaders and statesmen.

A descendant of the Alcmaeonids, Pericles was the son of a niece of Cleisthenes, whose reforms had laid the basis for the experiment in radical democracy that Pericles was not to realize. As early as 461 B.C., Pericles had espoused restricting the powers of the

*Above left, the Acropolis of Athens with the Parthenon to the right, the columns of the Propylaea in the center, and the small temple of Athena Nike between. A view of the interior of the Parthenon (above near right) and a closeup of one of its Doric column capitals (top right) reveal the ravages of time, but the temple remains indomitable (following pages).*

Areopagus, which had traditionally given elderly aristocrats a disproportionate influence in controlling the government. Under Pericles' direction, the Areopagus was divested of all but the most paltry powers and its political monopoly was effectively broken. Pericles went a step further. By reducing the property requirements for election to the high offices, he opened the channels of power to a larger group of citizens. Pericles also promoted the development of the large juries that not only sat in judgment over

most civil and criminal cases but also served as watchdogs over all government officials. The reform that brought Pericles the most scorn from his conservative opponents, however, was the institution of payment for service in the principal offices of state and on the juries. The conservatives regarded this new innovation as a disturbing way to bring middle-class citizens into participation in government. Working citizens had previously been denied a role in their democracy because they could not afford time away from their work. Conservatives also recognized that the poorest citizen could now supplement his meager income by continual service as a juror. So it was that Pericles could boast, according to the historian Thucydides, that poverty was no obstacle to participation in government.

Near the end of his own career—and what turned out to be the beginning of the end of imperial Athens—Pericles delivered a famous funeral oration in honor of those killed in the latest war with Sparta. Much of his speech was devoted to extolling the at-

*The Erechtheum (left) was a temple built by Mnesicles on the Acropolis between 430 and 408 B.C. on the site of many of the most sacred shrines of Athens. At the southwest corner is the Porch of the Caryatids (below far left), with six graceful maidens as columns.*

*Immediately below, the remains of the Stoa of Zeus, a portico built around 430 B.C. where Athenians conducted their commercial affairs. The marble seats (bottom), ca. 100 B.C., were reserved for dignitaries at the Theater of Dionysus in Athens.*

tainments of the state, but Pericles also praised the cultural state of Athens: "And when our work is finished, we Athenians are able to enjoy all kinds of recreation for our spirits. There are various contests and ceremonies throughout each year, and in our own homes we find a beauty and good taste that delight and distract us."

Pericles never forgot the role of culture in Athenian life. For two hundred years, Athens attracted an illustrious succession of poets, writers, dramatists, philosophers, and statesmen. Periclean Athens sponsored, for example, the work of such masters as the sculptor Phidias and nurtured the outstanding figures of the succeeding generation—Euripides the tragedian, Aristophanes the comic dramatist, Thucydides the historian, and Socrates the philosopher.

Pericles, of course, had his share of detractors, not only in his native Athens but also in the greater Greek world. After all, Pericles had used Delian League funds for public monuments in Athens, prompting one of his conservative opponents to compare his delegation of funds for the Acropolis to a prostitute's dressing up in expensive clothes. Indeed his expansionist policies won him as many critics as his beautification of Athens earned him allies. And Pericles, although his rule was legitimate, could be as ruthless as the most autocratic of tyrants in imposing his rule over subject peoples. When the island of Samos willfully ignored orders in a minor territorial dispute, Pericles himself sailed across the Aegean, established a new government, fined the inhabitants, and took hostages. After his return to Athens, a group of Sa-

mians released the hostages and recaptured the island. Pericles promptly returned to Samos, captured the island after a nine-month siege, and forced the Samians to destroy their walls and surrender their fleet. When Pericles boasted that Athens was "the school of the Greeks," there must have been many who listened with bitter irony.

In the years under Pericles, Athens was acknowledged as the leader of the Greek city-states. This position of preeminence was partly occasioned by the terms of the Thirty Years' Treaty signed in 445 B.C., which called for a suspension of open conflict between Athens and Sparta. The treaty was not equal to the task, however, and by 431 B.C., rivalries between the two city-states recommenced. The immediate cause of hostilities was a quarrel between Corcyra (the modern Corfu) and its mother-city, Corinth, that had continued for several years and soon involved more and more city-states. Corinth may have provided the excuse, but as Thucydides wrote: "The growth of the power of Athens, and the alarm which this inspired in Sparta, made war inevitable."

Of the two parties, the less bellicose was Sparta,

# Drama and theaters

Drama was a Greek invention. Developed from ancient religious rituals and mystery plays, drama was a public ceremony for the Athenians, financed partly by the state and in larger part by a tax on wealthy private citizens. Because Athenian tragedy was the focal point of the annual festival of Dionysus, attendance at the dramatic performances was a public duty as well as a sacred act.

The earliest Greek theaters consisted of an open hollow between steep slopes. Spectators sat on wooden seats along the slopes looking toward the stage, which was dug out of the earth itself. Later theaters imitated the hollow, seating audiences in a marble hemisphere that faced a stage and a backdrop of scenery.

*Athens of the fifth century B.C. produced four dramatists whose works still set the standard for world drama: the tragedians Aeschylus (above), Sophocles (left), and Euripides (below left); and Aristophanes, the comic playwright (below right).*

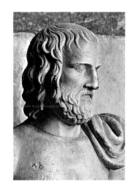

*Greek theaters began as natural slopes to which wooden seats were eventually added: they evolved into the great stone theaters such as that at Epidaurus (above) from the fourth or third century B.C. The plan of Athens' Theater of Dionysus (below left) shows its complex stage and backstage area.*

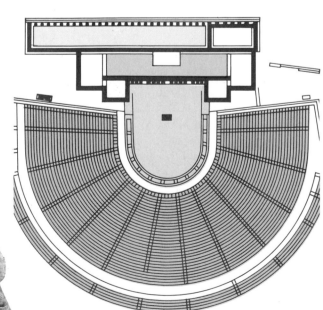

*Scenes from dramas were favorite subjects for vase painters. Far right, an episode on a krater from Euripides' Iphigenia in Tauris. The actors in a satyric drama (near right) have the more naturalistic costumes and masks characteristic of the plays that complemented the tragic trilogies.*

# Greek colonies

The foundation of colonies is one of the most characteristic acts of Greek civilization. The incentives for colonization came not only from imperialistic and commercial motives but were also a way of dealing with overpopulation, siphoning off the disaffected, and spreading Greek culture and influence around the Mediterranean world.

The first wave of colonists were Ionians, frightened or uprooted by the Dorian invasion. They crossed the Aegean in search of a second homeland on the coast of Asia Minor. The second, larger colonizing expedition had economic incentives. Between the eighth and the sixth centuries B.C., colonists were sent overseas from the Greek mainland to search for fertile lands. The emigration went by sea. Greek colonies were eventually established in all the Mediterranean lands with river banks, but always along the coast or near it.

Wherever they settled, the Greeks were prepared to subdue the local population, but the new cities they established were usually legally and economically independent. Shared cultural systems and mutual commercial interests assured many contacts and a generally amicable relationship with the Greek motherland. One unfortunate outcome of this loyalty was the occasional transfer of rivalries and hostilities from the founding cities to the colonies, which were drawn into the many virulent civil wars on the Greek mainland.

*Right, a map of the principal Greek communities in the ancient world. Among them were the city-states on Sicily, such as Acragas (better known as Agrigentum) where this stretch of Greek road (top left) remains, and Syracuse, at one time the greatest of all Greek cities. The ruins (center left) are from an altar of Gelon, the tyrant of Syracuse (485–478 B.C.) who inaugurated the city's ambitious development.*

*Wherever Greeks settled, they expressed their pride and prosperity in works that mirrored those of the homeland. At Poseidonia (better known as Paestum), in southern Italy, they built the Temple of Hera (bottom left), ca. 460 B.C. Below, the remains of Cyrene along the coast of what is now Libya. Founded by Greeks, Cyrene later became a Roman city, and most of these ruins are Roman. One of the most prosperous of all Greek cities was Miletus, in Asia Minor, where the entrance to the baths (below far right) remains.*

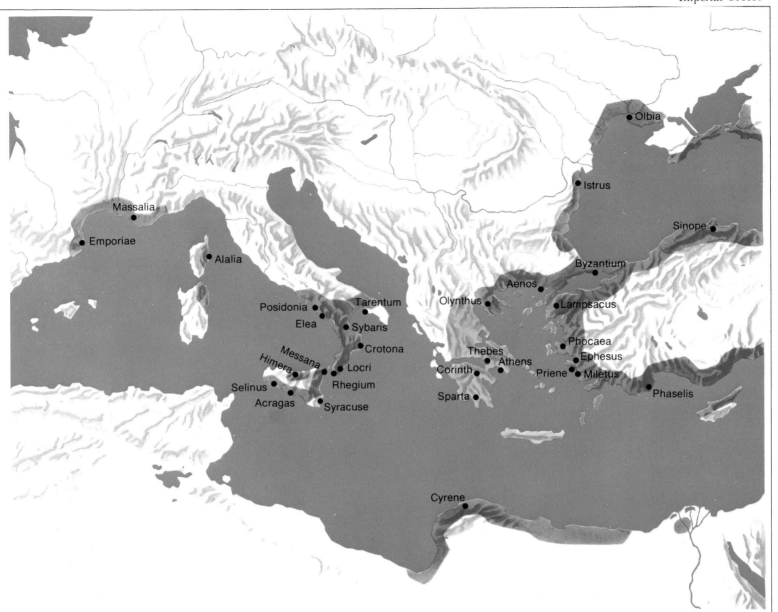

Massalia

Emporiae

Alalia

Posidonia
Elea
Tarentum
Sybaris
Crotona
Messana
Himera
Locri
Selinus
Rhegium
Acragas
Syracuse

Olynthus
Aenos
Thebes
Athens
Corinth
Priene
Sparta

Olbia

Istrus

Sinope

Byzantium

Lampsacus

Phocaea
Ephesus
Miletus

Phaselis

Cyrene

who had to contend with its growing and restive mass of helots. Sparta's financial position was also far inferior to that of Athens. There was every reason to believe that Sparta would settle for a return to the status quo. Meanwhile, with Pericles taking the lead, Athens appeared to be inviting confrontation. There was more than some truth to what a contemporary Corinthian said: "The Athenians are by nature incapable either of living a quiet life themselves or of allowing anyone else to do so."

When the Corinthian situation made war inevitable, Pericles persuaded the Athenians to withdraw to Attica behind the Long Walls which protected Athens and its port, Piraeus. At all costs, Pericles wanted to avoid a direct conflict with the far superior Spartan troops. Instead, he hoped to wear the enemy down by making a series of small raids from the sea. Pericles also counted on using the Athenian navy to cut off supplies from Sparta in the battle that was certain to come.

Technically, the first stage of what would become known as the Peloponnesian War began with an attack on Attica by the Spartan king Archidamus. The strategy devised by Pericles seemed successful, although those who were forced to abandon their land found small consolation in the success of the Athenian naval units. The tide soon turned. In 430 B.C., a plague swept the city and spread among the refugees crowded behind the Long Walls. In the face of the disaster, the Athenians demonstrated how fickle a people can be: They voted Pericles out of office and

fined him. But they had short memories. In 429 B.C., they were desperate for a leader and returned Pericles to office. Soon thereafter, he contracted the plague and died. "In what was nominally a democracy," Thucydides later wrote, "power was really in the hands of the first citizen."

The Athenians slowly recovered from the effects of the plague and followed Pericles' strategy of sniping at Sparta from the sea. Sparta made forays into Attica, but the Athenians managed to resist behind their Long Walls. After a series of inconclusive but costly engagements, the war wound down to a stalemate, and in 421 B.C., Sparta and Athens concluded a second treaty, the Peace of Nicias.

Forced neutrality may have brought a temporary cessation of hostilities between Sparta and Athens, but it did not insure equanimity between them and the rest of the Greek world. In fact, both city-states were saddled with increasingly restive allies. In 418 B.C., Sparta was drawn into open conflict with Argos in an attempt to reestablish its hegemony. Athens' immediate problem was Melos. In 416 B.C., an Athenian delegation invited the island of Melos to join the league, but the Melian leaders rejected their overtures. This resolute show of independence was not well-received by the Athenians, who seized the island, killed the adult males, and enslaved the women and children.

By 415 B.C., Athens had recovered some of its prosperity and confidence, but it was acutely conscious of the Spartan threat as well as its own dependence on

*Above, a bronze helmet dedicated to Hiero, tyrant of Syracuse, after leading the Greeks to victory. The armor (right) of a Greek warrior buried in Sicily includes his strigil, the curved scraper used to clean his body.*

The coin (above) was minted at Syracuse under the tyrant Gelon. At the end of the fifth century B.C., Syracuse began to build its great defensive walls that included the fortress of Euryalus (right).

Below, two coins issued by Taras (later Tarentum), in southern Italy—the only colony founded by Sparta. The Syracusans obtained the stone for their buildings from their own quarries (below right). It was in these quarries that the Athenians, after their defeat at Syracuse in 415 B.C., were kept prisoners until being sold into slavery.

grain supplies from abroad. When one of its allies in Sicily asked Athens for aid against Syracuse, the most powerful of the Greek city-states in the west, Athens saw an opportunity to solve two problems—to assure itself of grain from the rich fields of Sicily and to gain a western power base from which to apply pressure on Sparta.

The great armada that sailed from Athens seemed doomed from the start. Just as the fleet put to sea, one of its commanders, the brilliant (if erratic) and energetic (if unscrupulous) Alcibiades was accused of having committed various sacrileges against the official deities. A ship was later sent to return him to trial, but Alcibiades fled to Sparta. He convinced the Spartans to aid Syracuse and to invade Attica. By 414 B.C., Athens and Sparta were again at war. Worse was to follow.

After a great deal of vacillation, the Athenians blockaded Syracuse in 413 B.C. When the Athenian fleet became trapped in the harbor, however, its forces attempted to escape overland; those who survived were imprisoned in the quarries of Syracuse, and those who escaped were sold into slavery. Later it was said that the Syracusans spared those who could recite passages from the tragedies of Euripides—sweet revenge on the boast that Athens was "the school of

the Greeks."

The end of the Sicilian expedition was the single-most humiliating episode in the history of Athens. More significant for the Greek world, the expedition marked the dissolution of Athenian hegemony. Estimating that the Athenian forces were now enfeebled, Persia broke its treaty with Athens and reasserted its claim over the Greeks in Asia Minor. In memory of Athens' unpunished offenses to Persia, the Persians even paid the Spartans to continue hostilities against Athens. Not surprisingly, the democratic government that had brought about the questionable foreign ventures was virulently attacked, and in 411 B.C., a conservative oligarchy gained control.

The war with Sparta continued until 405 B.C., when a Spartan victory at the Hellespont deprived Athens of its fleet. Sparta then blockaded Athens to near starvation. In 404 B.C., the Athenians surrendered to the Spartans, who entered the city and demolished the Long Walls. The Athenian fleet was subsequently reduced to a few patrol boats, the Athenians' league was dissolved, and an oligarchy supported by Sparta, ruled by what the Athenians called the Thirty Tyrants, took over the government of Athens.

In an effort to fill the vacuum left by Athens,

*Left, a Roman copy of a statue, "The Wounded Warrior," the original attributed to Scopas, a Greek sculptor-architect active about 400–350 B.C. Its open emotionalism contrasts with the detached classical style.*

*Inside the Parthenon stood one of the most famous statues of antiquity, the Athena Parthenos of Phidias. Of ivory and gold, some fifty feet high, the original was lost, but it was frequently depicted and copied, as on the red jasper gem (above) from the Augustan period. One of the most successful replicas is the Varvakion Athena (right) (named after its finding place in Athens), a Roman copy of the second century A.D.*

159

Sparta immediately attempted to replace the Athenian system of government by imposing oligarchies on many of Athens' former allies and subjects. But Sparta had neither the heart nor the talent for foreign rule, and by 394 B.C., several major city-states—including Athens, Corinth, and Thebes—were allied in fighting Sparta. Sparta's domestic problems had meanwhile become even more serious, the helots becoming increasingly difficult to control. Sparta had also joined the Greeks of Asia Minor in yet another attempt to gain freedom from the Persians. But Sparta, with its deeply ingrained conservatism and inflexibility, lacked the instinct for empire building and was forced to capitulate to the Persians in 387 B.C. Asia Minor and Cyprus were returned to Persia under the treaty, the Athenians surrendered their alliances, and Sparta became Persia's law enforcement agency.

Sparta now had another opportunity to show it was capable of wielding a power bloc over the other city-states, but proved to be shortsighted, insensitive, and harsh. By 377 B.C., Athens tried to capitalize on the restlessness and anger among the other city-states by organizing the Second Athenian Confederacy. The real challenge to Sparta, however, came from Thebes. Under Epaminondas, the Thebans crushed the Spartans at the battle of Leuctra in 371 B.C., ending their supremacy. But Thebes was no more successful than Sparta in trying to create a harmonious federation, and when Epaminondas died in battle in 362 B.C., the Greek city-states again fell into disorder.

With the decline in Athens' political fortunes came a disenchantment at home. After the death of Pericles, many Athenians had begun to turn their energies to personal interest and gain, threatening the core of the democratic organization of Athens. Those who witnessed this moral and political decline must have recalled with some poignance the confident tone of Pericles' funeral oration: "We do not say that a man who takes no interest in politics is a man who

*The most revered Greek sculptor of the fourth century B.C. was Praxiteles. Among his most famous works was Hermes (left) dangling grapes before the infant Dionysus. Found at Olympia, it is generally considered to be an original. Another work attributed to Praxiteles is the relief (above) found at Mantinea, Greece, depicting three of the Muses.*

*Right, a form for casting a bronze leg for a statue. Found on the Acropolis, it dates from ca. 490 B.C. Freestanding bronze statues were made by the lost-wax process: a statue was first shaped in plaster or clay; its outside was covered with wax; another layer of clay was then applied; the wax was melted out; and liquid bronze was poured into the thin space to form the statue.*

minds his own business—we say he has no business at all in Athens."

The death of Socrates, the legendary philosopher who taught Plato and inspired many others, served as a comment on this troubled era. The circumstances leading up to his sentence have been muddled by conflicting and controversial accounts, but it is known that Socrates had been involved with the Thirty Tyrants installed by Sparta. The Athenians who overthrew them were uneasy about any reminders of the oligarchy they replaced, so they naturally viewed Socrates as a potential threat. In addition, Socrates had encouraged people to question conventional wisdom and was subsequently charged with encouraging religious impiety. Brought to trial in 399 B.C., he was found guilty by a vote of 281 to 220. In the words of his accusers, he was "guilty of not believing in the gods in which the polis believes and of introducing other, new divinities. He is also guilty of corrupting the young. The penalty is death." The

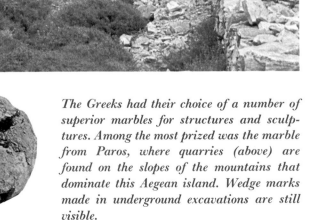

*The Greeks had their choice of a number of superior marbles for structures and sculptures. Among the most prized was the marble from Paros, where quarries (above) are found on the slopes of the mountains that dominate this Aegean island. Wedge marks made in underground excavations are still visible.*

# Containers of liquids

The two leading Greek exports, wine and olive oil, were placed in pottery jars for sale. These painted jars assumed standardized shapes and sizes depending on their contents and uses.

The paintings on Athenian vases of the sixth to fourth century B.C. were in either black-figure or red-figure style. In black-figure the subject was painted with a liquid clay that turned black in firing. Backgrounds were left the color of the clay, and details were scratched into the black.

Red-figure is exactly the reverse. The background was painted black and the subject left in the reddish clay color. Details were applied with a brush, giving the artist much more flexibility.

Frequently the subject matter on vases relates to wine production and consumption, but athletics, dancing, and other leisure activities were also common. Such vase paintings provide an intriguing perspective on the lives and habits of the early Greeks.

*The basic water carrier of the Greeks was the hydria, like those used by the women in the kylix painting (below left). Below right, two measuring cups and a clepsydra, which allowed water to drip out of the base into a similar container below, thereby "clocking" a specific time.*

*Above left, the satyr Silenus painted inside a kylix, expressing the ecstasy of wine drinking. The Greeks generally avoided the intoxicating power of wine but appreciated it at times, as in this banquet scene (above) painted in a tomb at Paestum.*

The krater (left) was painted by the Greek Polygnotos, active about 475–447 B.C., with a traditional scene of the giants fighting the gods. Once water and wine were mixed in a krater, the drink was poured into a small kylix (right), convenient for drinking. Below left, an early geometrically ornamented pitcher for pouring oil. A reminder that ancient Greeks had more mundane concerns than wine drinking is this bathtub (below), a sit-down type, from a colony in Sicily. Greeks were not ignorant of personal hygiene, although they did not emphasize bathing as did the Romans.

*Above, the arcaded road leading to the theater at Ephesus (below), one of the earliest and greatest of the Ionian Greek cities in Asia Minor. Like many of the Greeks' overseas communities, Ephesus flourished long after the decline of the mainland Greek city-states. Such theaters were often greatly transformed during the Hellenistic and Roman periods.*

*Above, the Ecclesiasterion, or council house (ca. 200 B.C.), of the Greek colony at Priene in Asia Minor. Priene was not founded until about 350 B.C., long after most of the major Ionian cities, but as this structure and the regular plan of the rest of the city suggest, even at this time the Greeks were intent on maintaining and transplanting their forms of architecture and government. The structure had seating for perhaps six or seven hundred persons. Visible here are the stepped stone benches and, at center, the altar for dedicatory offerings.*

philosopher could easily have shown contrition and requested a fine or exile in exchange. Instead, he adhered uncompromisingly to his own precepts and drank the hemlock poison prescribed by his sentence. Although Socrates undoubtedly began as one of Athenian democracy's finest creations, he ended as one of its victims.

In the decades that followed, Athens and Sparta both had to contend with factional quarrels within their own city-states, the ever-present enmity of Persia, and now, a new threat—the people to the north of Greece, the Macedonians. Not quite dismissible as barbarians yet not true Greeks, the Macedonians were simple, hardy tribesmen. Peasants for the most part, but with an elite of equestrians, they had been ruled since 413 B.C. by their own kings. In 359 B.C., Philip II ascended the throne and moved quickly to reform the government. He also transformed his armed forces into the most professional of the day, with a heavy cavalry, flexible infantry, and swift ships.

Philip then began to expand the kingdom of Macedonia, openly seizing territory and cities that belonged to city-states on the mainland. In Athens, as yet untouched by Philip by 350 B.C., the great orator Demosthenes began to make a series of speeches, the *Philippics,* warning his fellow citizens of the imminent threat from the Macedonians. Athens and other city-states eventually recognized the truth of Demosthenes' warnings but were unable to stop their bickering in time to organize an effective resistance. In 338 B.C., the Macedonians defeated a major force of Athenians and Thebans at Chaeronea, in central Greece. Philip proceeded diplomatically by organizing his own League of Corinth by which he ruled Greece. In one sense, the new league was the unifying force that the Greeks had always been striving to create. In another sense, this final unification at the hands of a foreigner extinguished the hope that Greece would ever achieve peace from within.

The Greeks had not been defeated by the Persians nor really by the Macedonians. They had defeated themselves by their inability to rise above their chronic factionalism. Athens and Sparta, the two greatest Greek states, had ironically done more than all the others combined to bring about Greece's downfall. Their destiny was perhaps best expressed by the historian Thucydides:

If Sparta were to be destroyed and there remained only the temples and the foundations of the buildings, later generations would find it hard to believe that she had been so powerful. . . . Whereas if the same thing were to happen to Athens, from the

*The monument (above) is a decree by the Ecclesia of Athens in 405 B.C. to honor Samos for its aid in the war against Sparta. Below, remains of the palace at Thebes, which dominated Greece for about a decade.*

appearance of the city posterity might judge her to have been twice as powerful as she actually is.

After Chaeronea, an empire appeared that would overshadow the grandest ambitions of Athens and the military power of Sparta. The mission was to be achieved by King Philip's son, a student of Aristotle and commander of the Macedonian cavalry at Chaeronea—a young man by the name of Alexander.

*Right, the stele of Aristonautes, attributed to Scopas, ca. 330 B.C., which conveys the spirit of an age when Greece felt threatened. The threat came from Macedonia under Philip II, whose coin (facing page, below) reflects his name ("lover of horses") and the power of his cavalry. After the Macedonians defeated the allied Greeks in 338 B.C., the Thebans erected a formidable lion (facing page, above)—a sad irony, for it marked the end of the independent city-states of classical Greece.*

# Photography Credits

*Borromeo:* p. 54 / *British Museum:* p. 26, p. 28 top, p. 30 top, p. 31 top and bottom left / *Costa:* p. 55, p. 77 right, p. 85 bottom left and right, p. 114 bottom left and right, p. 115 bottom left, p. 132 center, p. 133 top right, p. 167 bottom / *Dulevant:* p. 43 / *Ferrari A.:* p. 39 bottom left, p. 42, p. 73 top right / *Ferrari M.:* p. 161 right / *Fiore:* p. 10 bottom right, p. 84, p. 94 bottom right, p. 106 bottom left and right, p. 154 center and bottom, p. 155 bottom left, p. 163 bottom left, p. 164 top left / *Foto 2000:* p. 157 top / *Frezzato:* p. 47 bottom left, p. 64 top, p. 82 top and bottom right, p. 83, p. 85 top / *Interfoto-F. Rausch:* pp. 58–59 / *Leigheb:* p. 11, pp. 50–51, pp. 78–79 / *Magnum-Lessing:* p. 30 bottom right, p. 31 bottom right, p. 32, p. 33 bottom, p. 38, p. 40, p. 41 top and bottom left, p. 46, p. 47 right, p. 49, p. 66 top right, p. 67 top left, p. 72, p. 73 bottom left and right, p. 98 center, p. 99, p. 101 left, p. 109 bottom right, p. 114 top, p. 115 bottom right, p. 131 bottom, p. 133 top left, p. 144 bottom left / *Mairani:* p. 129 left, p. 132 top / *Marka:* p. 146 / *Pedone:* p. 16 left, p. 23 bottom and top right, p. 24 top, p. 28 bottom left, p. 39, p. 53 top / *Pellegrini:* p. 10 top, p. 13, p. 47 top left, p. 60 bottom, p. 80 center, p. 164 top right and bottom / *Pubbliaerfoto:* pp. 104–105, p. 108 top, p. 136 right, pp. 140–141, p. 142 top / *Pucciarelli:* p. 96 top, p. 97 top, p. 98 top left, bottom left, and right, p. 100, p. 111 bottom, p. 117 top, p. 118, p. 119 bottom right, p. 120 bottom, p. 121 top right and bottom, p. 124 bottom, p. 129 right, p. 130, p. 133 bottom, p. 134 right second and third pictures from top, p. 135 left third picture from top, p. 138 bottom left and right, p. 139 top and bottom right, p. 144 top right and bottom right, p. 145 top right, p. 150 center right and bottom right, p. 152 bottom left and center right, p. 153 bottom, p. 162 bottom left, center, and bottom right / *Ricatto:* p. 107 / *Ricciarini-Bevilacqua:* p. 17, p. 24 bottom, p. 27, p. 34 bottom, p. 65 bottom right, p. 66 left, p. 67 top right and bottom left, p. 69 center left and bottom left, p. 76 top and bottom left, p. 125 top right / *Ricciarini-Cirani:* p. 12, p. 56, p. 61 bottom right, p. 65 left, p. 66 bottom right, p. 70 / *Ricciarini-Prato:* p. 69 center right, p. 69 bottom right, p. 123 / *Ricciarini-Simion:* p. 33 top, p. 35, pp. 36–37, p. 89, p. 110 top, p. 116 bottom, p. 127 top and bottom left, p. 134 bottom, p. 137, p. 139 center right, p. 151 / *Ricciarini-Tomsich:* p. 28 bottom right, p. 41 bottom right, pp. 74–75, p. 90 bottom, p. 91, p. 97 bottom left, p. 106 top, p. 109 bottom left, p. 111 bottom right, p. 113 top, p. 116 bottom, p. 125 bottom, p. 138 top left, p. 147 top, p. 162 top / *Rizzoli:* p. 29 top left, p. 29 bottom and center right, pp. 44–45, p. 77 left, p. 90 top, p. 94 bottom left and right, p. 96 bottom, p. 101 right, p. 102, p. 103 top, p. 109 top right and center left, p. 111 bottom left, p. 115 top right and center right, p. 119 bottom left, p. 121 left, p. 122, p. 125 top left, p. 128 top, p. 131 top, p. 132 bottom, p. 135 left first, second, and fourth pictures from top, p. 134 right first and fourth pictures from top, p. 135 right fourth picture from top, p. 136 left, p. 142 bottom, p. 143, p. 145 center and bottom, p. 150 top, p. 152 center left, p. 156 top, p. 157, p. 159, p. 160 left, p. 163 center left, p. 165 top, p. 166, p. 167 top / *Roger-Viollet:* p. 82 bottom left / *Scala:* p. 103 center and bottom, p. 112 top left, top right, and bottom, p. 113 bottom, p. 116 top left and right, p. 117 bottom left and right, p. 126, p. 127 top right and bottom right, p. 156 bottom, p. 162 top, p. 162 bottom right, p. 163 center right, / *Rossdeutscher:* p. 155 bottom right / *S.E.F.:* p. 29 top right, p. 61 center right, p. 64 bottom, p. 65 top right, p. 67 center right and bottom right, p. 68, p. 69 top left and right, p. 71, p. 76 bottom right, p. 128 bottom / *Sheridan:* p. 87, p. 147 bottom, pp. 148–149 / *Stierlin:* p. 9, p. 18, p. 19, pp. 20–21, p. 22, p. 52, p. 53 bottom left and right, p. 57, p. 62, p. 63, p. 80 bottom, p. 81 / *Titus:* p. 16 right, p. 23 top left, p. 25, p. 34 top left and right, p. 48, p. 60 top, p. 61 top left and right, p. 80 top, p. 94 top, p. 95, p. 135 right first three pictures from top, p. 98 top right, p. 108 bottom right, p. 111 top, p. 120 top, p. 124 top and center, p. 139 bottom left, p. 150 bottom left, p. 153 top, p. 154 top, p. 158, p. 160 right, p. 165 bottom / *Vergani:* p. 10 bottom left

# Index